of MINISTERS *and* MEN

A Call to Decentralize the Body of Christ

GERIZIM

Of Ministers and Men:
A Call to Decentralize the Body of Christ

Copyright © 2000, 2015, 2017 Don McIntosh
Gerizim Publishing, Houston, Texas
www.gerizimpublishing.com

ISBN-13: 978-0692927588
ISBN-10: 0692927581

Cover illustration "Mice in Council" by Nora Fry, from *Aesop's Fables*, London: J. Coker & Co., Ltd., 1929.

Unless otherwise noted, Scripture references are from the New King James Version of the Holy Bible. Copyright © 1982, Thomas Nelson, Inc. Used by permission.

Dedicated to:

Tricia, my lovely wife of twenty-seven years
and best friend on earth.

"And who is a chosen man that I may appoint over her?
For who is like Me? Who will arraign Me?
And who is that shepherd who will stand against Me?"

-- Jeremiah 50:44

Contents

An Urgent Call

LIKE ALL WRITERS, I believe that what I have to say is worth saying, that is, important. I have rewritten this little book yet again for the same reason I wrote the initial draft some eighteen years ago: because I felt called and compelled to do so. That God would call a man to such a task makes sense, given that God loves His church even more than men love their religious traditions.

Yet a more urgent call confronts us. Although we have all selfishly, stubbornly sinned against the God who created us, that same God in love and mercy now calls us to escape the judgment our sins deserve and experience eternal life in Jesus Christ. "Repent," said Jesus, "for the kingdom of heaven is at hand." (Matt. 4:17). God calls us to literally *change our minds* about sin and selfishness, and seek life in Him instead.

This is an urgent message not only because life is short – often unexpectedly so – but because history itself is drawing to a close. Biblical signs of the "last days" are all around us: the physical restoration of the Jews to their ancient homeland following centuries of wandering and persecution; widespread apostasy from the faith; exponential growth of knowledge and technology; blood moons, UFO sightings and other "great signs from heaven;" growing frequency and intensity of earthquakes, famines and diseases; gradual global unification of political and monetary systems; and an expanding host of militant radical-Islamic forces on a mission to first annihilate the tiny state of Israel and then conquer the rest of the world in the name of religion. The time to repent is now.

-- *D.M.*

Preface to the Latest Edition

The best-laid plans of mice and men, so often go awry.

-- Robert Burns, "To a Mouse"

For no other foundation can anyone lay than that which is laid, which is Jesus Christ.

-- 1 Corinthians 3:11

HAVING WRITTEN the first edition of this little book to explore questions of structure and leadership in the church, and having written two other editions to defend and expand upon the themes sketched out in the first, I recently felt the need to revise it yet again. Now in light of the fact that none of the previous editions were widely published, let alone bestsellers, one might wonder why I would bother with a *fourth* edition.

Here are a few reasons: First, the structure-related problems I wrote about many years ago and address again in the present volume have not gone away. Thus there is an ongoing need for messages like this one to be heard.

Second, in recent years there has been an increasing interest in reformation – even revolution – in the church, as the surging house church movement would suggest. According to a 2006 study by George Barna, involvement with house churches rose 8% (from 1% to 9% of American adults) in the previous decade.[1] Another Barna study from 2009 indicated that 22-24% of adults participated

---

[1] "House Church Involvement Is Growing," *Barna Group*, June 19, 2006. https://www.barna.org/barna-update/organic-church.

in a non-traditional church during the previous month.[2] In other words this *simple* church or *organic* church movement, as it is also called, is growing fast, which means that this book's message is much more "culturally relevant" now than when I first wrote it.

Additionally I am writing to temper a message written previously in much frustration, indignation and even defiance. The experiences of some eighteen years since the first publication have softened my heart toward my brethren still in the traditional-institutional church, and for that I am grateful to God. One of my arguments here is that the church finds its expression in *numerous* ways, not just "the way we've always done things." But the argument cuts both ways: I know from experience that countless sincere, spiritual members of the body of Christ gather in more traditional church organizations, right along with those of us who are pursuing the close-knit fellowship and mutual accountability that describes the New Testament church.

Bearing in mind that love is the highest spiritual virtue (1 Cor. 13:13), and with the love of God having been "poured out" in my heart by the Holy Spirit (Rom. 5:5), I can now honestly say that I hold no antipathy toward my brothers and sisters in more traditional churches. After all, I was led to Jesus through the evangelistic efforts of a hierarchical church organization, through which I was then trained and instructed in serious discipleship for around fifteen years. It would be evil and foolish for me to now despise that ministry. Undoubtedly God has managed to use each of various ecclesiastical forms, just as he manages to use each of us as sinful individuals, for his own glory. I for one, however, no longer function well in the pastor-centered model, for reasons to be explained in the following pages, so that I for one am grateful to God for alternative models.

---

[2] "How Many People Really Attend a House Church? Barna Study Finds It Depends on the Definition," *Barna Group*, August 31, 2009. https://www.barna.org/barna-update/organic-church.

Therefore I would like to expand upon the New Testament concept of "diversity of gifts" a bit, and suggest that in the Christian church there is equally a *diversity of venues and structures*. Though I personally advocate the house church model, I also realize the importance of remaining humbly connected to the larger body of Christ. As John Fenn has observed, many in the house church movement are not just occasionally critical of, but even dead-set against, the traditional church: "But," he says, "there is great value in going to hear a speaker or a teacher in a traditional church.... After all, 3,000 people were gathered to hear Peter at Pentecost!"[3]

Given this diversity, my current approach to the subject is less *de*structive and more *con*structive. In the interests of goodwill I have softened the language, removed criticisms of specific leaders and organizations, and generally left out the more reactionary elements from prior editions. Though a wealth of useful and relevant material has been published since 1999,[4] my cited references remain for the most part as they were then. I have, however, changed the title to *Of Ministers and Men*, which sounds a bit less provocative than *Of Pastors and Kings* (the original title), and more to the point: Indeed one of my basic contentions remains that in the church as envisioned by Christ and the apostles *all men are ministers*.[5] Also I have added an Appendix ("Meeting House to House") to this latest edition, outlining some of the practical nuts-and-bolts issues of gathering in homes.

---

[3] John Fenn, *Return of the First Church* (Indianapolis: Dog Ear Publishing, 2007), p. 195.

[4] The original edition of the one book said by many to have unofficially "launched" the modern house church movement, *Pagan Christianity* by Frank Viola, was published in 2002.

[5] The same holds for all *women*, whose ministerial roles in the church are addressed briefly in the Appendix.

I would like to express my gratitude, first and always to the Lord Jesus Christ himself, for redeeming me and for "putting me into the ministry" despite my past sins (1 Tim. 12). I am grateful also to my wife Tricia for her faithful companionship during good and bad times alike, and to my children, Vance and Chloe, for the sheer joy they bring to my life. Also I should thank Dr. Johnson C. Philip, my mentor at Trinity School of Apologetics and Theology, for being such a tireless and encouraging example of the kind of leadership I promote in the pages to follow; and Herb Drake of House Church Central,[6] for providing resources both informative and inspirational for actually putting house church into action.

While certainly not a *perfect* church model or the answer to every problem addressed in this book, house church ministry has at least provided an outlet for putting into practice what I have long believed in the way of every-member participation and the unrestrained exercise of spiritual gifts. As we meet in homes we are free to enjoy worship, fellowship and ministry in a way so many of us never quite have before. My family and I are blessed to experience today what we once believed was forever locked away in the record of ancient history: "And they continued steadfastly in the apostles' doctrine and fellowship, in the breaking of bread, and in prayers. Then fear came upon every soul, and many wonders and signs were done through the apostles. Now all who believed were together, and had all things in common…" (Acts 2:42-44).

Don McIntosh
Houston, Texas
October 2017

---

[6] To find out more about meeting in homes or to find a house church in your area, please see the House Church Central website: www.hccentral.com/.

Concerning Structure (of This Book)

IT ONLY MAKES SENSE that a book about structure would be sensibly organized. In keeping with one of the main premises of my thesis here, that "form follows function," I've organized the text around the functions of various parties in the church.

Chapter One is essentially a brief critique of the traditional top-down, hierarchical or pyramid church structure, which is contrasted with the much more loosely structured model depicted in the New Testament.

With the understanding established that leadership ministry extends far beyond the role of the pastor, Chapters Two through Six examine the roles of the local assembly, elders, deacons, and then what is commonly called the "fivefold ministry" of Eph. 4:11 – apostles, prophets, evangelists, pastors and teachers. Since I address pastoral leadership separately in Chapter Three (concerning the elders), my treatment of this latter set of functions could be called "fourfold" instead.[7]

Following a critique of the institutional church and analyses of individual ministerial functions in Scripture, I attempt to put everything back together in Chapter Seven by sketching out the rough outlines of how the church might be expected to operate when taking into account the material in the rest of the book.

---

[7] Note that some scholars and commentators combine "pastors" and "teachers" into a single function to indicate a fourfold rather than fivefold ministry (something like the approach I take here), while others may recall John Calvin's old fourfold division of pastors, doctors, elders, and deacons – where the "doctor" is a university-trained intellectual and doctrinal guardian of the church.

I. A Conspicuous Absence: The Search for Church Structure in the New Testament

The accumulation of all powers, legislative, executive, and judiciary, in the same hands, whether of one, a few, or many, and whether hereditary, self-appointed or elective, may justly be pronounced the very definition of tyranny.

-- James Madison, *Federalist No. 47*

For as the body is one and has many members, but all the members of that body, being many, are one body, so also is Christ.

-- 1 Corinthians 12:12

THEIR DOCTRINES DIFFER, as do their dress and decorum. Some churches stress the importance of sympathetic virtues such as forgiveness, compassion and redemption. Others dwell more on the "meatier" issues of obedience, commitment, and responsibility. Some emphasize legalistic particulars – baptism, tithing, observing the Sabbath, speaking in tongues, or even allegiance to their particular denomination or movement – as necessary attendants to salvation. Others insist that salvation is attained by grace alone through faith in Jesus alone – *sola gratia, sola fide.* (Both sides are often suspicious of the others' motives, and just as often unwilling to concede that there are probably at least a few folks going to heaven from the "other" side.) Some are highly motivated to win the world by preaching; others hope to influence their communities by ministering to the poor and needy. (Both are involved in valid expressions of the gospel.) Some worship loudly with music and celebration; others are more subdued.

Common to almost all Christian churches, however, is the centrality of the pastor. Walk into any church meeting on a Sunday morning, and you will typically find a man speaking from behind a pulpit. Whether he is esteemed or despised, admired or ignored, the pastor is the structural hub of the modern church, and his sermon is the vehicle he uses for bringing correction and maturity to the body of Christ. While he graces the pulpit there is to be no talking, whispering or giggling – in short, no real fellowship. (Someone once noted that the only fellowship to be experienced in the church nowadays is with the back of someone's head!)

In many places the pastor alone is considered qualified to minister to the church, so any work done by others is that which he chooses to delegate. He may have on his staff an assistant pastor, an outreach director, a youth leader, a council or board of directors, a handful of musicians, some Bible study leaders, and a host of others fulfilling ministry functions in the church; but everyone understands that the whole program is pretty much his baby, and consequently all are answerable to him.

Historians attribute this remarkable uniformity of structure to Martin Luther and the Reformers. Luther, of course, revolutionized the church by restoring the gospel message to the common man. He rightly contended that every individual had the right to salvation by faith, without relying on legalistic works or the approval of popes or priests. He refused to communicate the Word in Latin to a German-speaking populace, limiting access of the practical truth of Scripture to a priestly class. Instead he published an accessible German translation himself. Indeed, Luther maintained that every Christian was part of a universal "priesthood of believers" enjoying direct access to God. He condemned the sale of indulgences, by which parishioners could literally buy salvation for their loved ones supposedly burning in purgatory and patiently awaiting their deliverance. Practically alone, Martin Luther boldly resisted the excesses of the papacy, holding them up to the light of God's Word for all the world to see.

Yet the Protestant Reformation is a striking study in irony. For in present-day churches, Luther has become a bit of an icon. His views, along with those of John Calvin and the other reformers, have been treated as the final word on many issues of leadership and structure in the church. Whether it was Luther's intention or not, almost every Protestant Christian church since the Reformation has without question (and without biblical justification) adopted the Lutheran-Calvinist pattern of preacher, pulpit and parishioner. Historian Vivian Green writes of the reformed churches: "They had a structured ministry...but the minister was no longer a priest who mediated between God and man, but a preacher expounding the Word of God...."[8]

That is, while priest gave way to preacher, the essential structure remained intact. Luther may have resisted a rigid ecclesiastical hierarchy, but he actually established another. He spoke out against spiritual gurus accountable to none, and in the process became one. Luther's opinions – like those of the popes before him – became a fixed, if ironic, standard of doctrine in the church: "Over Lutheranism [i.e., the Reformation] the spirit of Martin Luther hovered as the Titan among the reformers."[9]

The upshot of all this is that Luther's work remains largely incomplete. James Rutz calls it the "2/3 Reformation:" "The 'priesthood of the believer,' the central goal of the Reformation, has been restored only theologically, not practically. It still remains mainly on paper. In very important ways, our churches remain closed to laymen."[10] Viola and Barna more recently expressed the same thought: "What the Reformers failed to do was to recover the corporate dimension of the believing priesthood. They restored the

---

[8] Vivian Green, *A New History of Christianity* (New York: Continuum, 1996), p. 156.

[9] Green, p. 133.

[10] James H. Rutz, *The Open Church: How to Bring Back the Exciting Life of the First Century Church* (Auburn, Maine: Seedsowers, 1992), p. 13.

doctrine of the believing priesthood soteriologically – i.e., as it related to salvation. But they failed to restore it ecclesiologically – i.e., as it related to the church."[11]

All this suggests that there is still a sizeable gulf fixed between clergy and laity, between minister and flock. And indeed, it seems that in many churches the pastor's job is to preach; ours is but to listen. His is to counsel; ours is to listen. His is to teach; ours is to listen. This arrangement is as unbiblical as it is unfortunate. Luther, it turns out, merely replaced the priesthood with the pastorate.

I don't mean to sound ungrateful. Thanks to the reformers, believers are now free to pray to God and read the Bible for themselves. They are not, however, generally free to preach, teach, prophesy, offer counsel to their brethren or contribute at all to the direction of the church. (Such duties are strictly reserved for the pastor.) With tongue in cheek, Os Guinness celebrates what amounts to the bottom-line impact of the Reformation on modern-day churches: "The old priesthood is dead! Long live the new power-pastors and pundit-priests!"[12] Guinness' point is well taken – that pastors are still, by and large, the extra-biblical "mediators between God and men" denounced by the reformers.

What explains this ongoing state of counter-reform in the church? I believe it derives from two factors. First, there is the absence of clearly formulated patterns of structure in the New Testament. Think about it. How can the church really be "re-formed" if no one knows how it was formed in the first place? There is precious little in the Gospels, the letters of Paul, or even the book of Acts which describes the administrative functions of pastors and others in the church. Most of the leadership admonitions made by Jesus, Paul and Peter have to do with character, not

---

[11] Frank Viola & George Barna, *Pagan Christianity?* (Carol Stream, Ill: Tyndale, 2012), p. 106.

[12] Os Guinness, *Dining with the Devil* (Grand Rapids: Baker Book House, 1993, p. 72).

with securing a place on the organizational chart. Jesus proclaimed loudly and often that leadership begins with servanthood. He of course set the example Himself, serving others, washing the disciples' feet, and finally sacrificing His very life on a cross of crucifixion. "For even the Son of Man did not come to be served, but to serve, and to give His life a ransom for men" (Mark 10:45).

In similar fashion, Paul argued that the legitimacy of the local pastor was based not on his charisma or his level of education, but on his testimony and his character: "A bishop then must be blameless" (1 Tim. 3:2). Peter addressed the necessities of humility, motive and exampleship: "...not as being lords over those entrusted to you, but being examples to the flock" (1 Pet. 5:3). What these apostles do not mention is how the pastor executes the duties of his office in day-to-day matters confronting the church. They do not say how much the pastor should decide or how much he should delegate. They do, however, drop a few curious hints that pastors do not lead the churches all by themselves, but alongside others.

Likewise, the book of Acts offers but a sketchy outline of the structural development of the church. It records the ministry of evangelists like Paul and Philip, and the appointment of deacons like Stephen. In some cases the roles overlap, as when Philip the deacon becomes Philip the evangelist in a moment of obedience to the instruction of an angel. Only James in the church of Jerusalem can be recognized as a prominent leader in the local church, while the pastor (if there was just one) of the more effective and outgoing church at Antioch remains nameless. It seems safe to say that in Acts the church was relatively unstructured and decentralized. Chapter Thirteen describes the Antioch church, led by a diverse group of "prophets and teachers," fasting and praying, and in response to the Holy Spirit, sending out Paul and Barnabas to the mission field. There was apparently no policy, no procedure, no paperwork, and no pastoral approval required to make this move. The only leader of this particular act of the apostles was the Holy Spirit.

Those holding to the "episcopal" or hierarchical theory of church structure should be advised to read Acts 15, in which all parties – apostles, elders, and "all the multitude of the believers" – converged in Jerusalem to debate the problem of legalism spreading among new converts. James, the local pastor, actually had the last word, using his considerable influence to modify Peter's recommendation that Gentile converts be fully embraced by the church, adding a number of specific requirements for the Gentiles not recorded elsewhere in the New Testament. While such converts need not be circumcised, said James, they should be instructed to "abstain from things polluted by idols, from sexual immorality, and from blood" (Acts 15:20). *Hard Sayings of the Bible* notes the potential for confusion in the council:

> But in spite of his apparent agreement [with the apostles], James added the stipulation of this verse both in his advice to the council and in his letter to the Gentile believers…. Is this a case, then, in which Paul won the first round but was knocked out in the end? Does this not contradict all that Paul stood for?[13]

Now I am not trying to say (nor are the authors of *Hard Sayings*) that the ruling of the Jerusalem council was a mistake, for the apostles' comments on it are affirmative: "It seemed good to the Holy Spirit, and to us" (v. 28). My point is merely that the ruling was the result of a process of informal deliberation rather than of apostolic decree. (Even so, at was not a binding ordinance, for it had been altered still further by the time Paul wrote his letters to the Romans and Corinthians, in which he left the issue of dietary customs to be decided by the conscience of the individual [Rom. 14; 1 Cor. 8] .) Left unanswered was the question of just who is supposed to be in charge – pastors like James, apostles like Paul, or the general assembly of believers.

---

[13] Walter C. Kaiser, Peter H. Davids, and F.F. Bruce, *Hard Sayings of the Bible* (Madison, Wisconsin: Intervarsity, 1996), p. 528.

It would be easy to conclude from all this that the church had, and therefore should have, no structure at all. This would be a false and presumptuous conclusion. The apostle Paul was certainly no advocate of chaos. "Let all things be done decently and in order," he reminded the super-spiritual Corinthian church (1 Cor. 14:40). What I find interesting in this context is that Paul wrote this letter to the entire church, not to "the pastor" (who by the way is not mentioned), and exhorted them to devise some sort of order for their disheveled services. We get the picture of a church that is called to govern itself as the need arises. There are no job descriptions or flow charts.

The evidence suggests that God has given the church a few specific commands, a specific commission, some specific callings, and then left the lesser job of organization to the church itself. He tells us exactly what He wants done, but not exactly how to do it. All He has left us is the record of history and a smattering of clues throughout the letters of Paul and the book of Acts. Williston Walker speaks for the entire community of historians in *A History of the Christian Church*: "No question in church history has been more darkened by controversy than that of the origin and development of church officers, and none is more difficult, owing to the scantiness of the evidence that has survived."[14]

This conspicuous absence of structure in the New Testament has led the church, I believe, to simply fall back on the Old Testament pattern of prophets, judges and kings. This may be considered the second major factor explaining the glut of overbearing and unbalanced leadership in the church today. For lack of anything better, most pastors have structured their ministries after that of Moses, Joshua, Samuel, Saul (the bad, backslidden pastor) and David (the good, spiritual pastor). At least this way, churches can correctly claim that they have chosen a biblical pattern. Scholars such as John E. Johnson state matter-of-factly that the Old Testa-

---

[14] Williston Walker, *A History of the Christian Church*, rev. ed. (New York: Charles Scribner's Sons, 1970), p. 39.

ment is now the dominant paradigm for leadership in New Testament churches:

> By the time of Luther and Calvin, the three offices of prophet, priest, and king became the central organizing principle of Protestant Christological teaching, the manner in which to describe the ministry of Christ. These also serve as the central organizing structure of the pastoral office.[15]

The many New Testament references to the "kingdom of God" seem to support such a view, that God as King has no use for other forms of church government such as representative democracy. So the theology is understandable. It is still wrong, however, as we will see.

Arguably the adherence to a monarchical leadership model can be traced to a single incident back in the Old Testament. Samuel was the last of the judges. As the record of Scripture indicates, he was a good man and a powerful prophet. Unfortunately, his sons chose not to adopt his spiritual vision or his moral convictions. When at last Samuel was ready to retire, the people of Israel came upon a not-so-bright idea for replacing him: They would jettison God's plan of leadership for them in favor of one modeled after the surrounding nations. They clamored for a king.

Samuel took this as a personal affront. But God took it even more personally, expressing to Samuel his explicit disapproval of Israel's obstinate worldliness: "...for they have not rejected you, but they have rejected Me, that I should not reign over them" (1 Sam. 8:7). Samuel then warned the nation of the abuses that would necessarily follow. Don't miss the point raised by this bit of Bible history: God never endorsed monarchy as an acceptable form of

---

[15] Roy B. Zuck, ed., *Vital Church Issues: Examining Principles and Practices in Church Leadership* (Grand Rapids: Kregel Resources, 1998), p. 122.

ecclesiastical government. He has always desired to rule over the church Himself, as only He can do.

So it is to this day. God longs to once again take His place as Ruler of the church, which after all He purchased with His own blood. In the search for New Testament church structure, it seems that a good place for us to start would be to once again recognize the undisputed Lordship of Christ – above that of pastors, priests, or popes. This is the essence of Christianity, submitting to the final authority of the King of kings. He alone is "the head of all principality and power" (Col. 2:10) and "head of the church" (Eph. 5:23). It follows that any man who claims to be the "headship" of the church is actually resisting the exclusive authority of Christ. Missionary leader J. Oswald Sanders describes the problem of authoritarianism as a "rapidly developing trend" in the church, which "easily leads to a...behavioral pattern that usurps the authority of the Head of the Church, grieves the Holy Spirit, and robs the believer of his personal right of decision-making."[16]

The elevation of the pastoral office in the modern church is apparently little more than an extension of the Israelites' longing to serve a human king in the flesh rather than serve Christ by faith. This is an old habit that the church has never been able to completely break. In the first century, for instance, the Pharisees towered over the people of Palestine as a ruling clique, demanding preferential treatment in everything from privileges and perks to flattering titles. Jesus explicitly condemned their spiritual "superiority complex":

"They love the best places at feasts, the best seats at the synagogue, greetings in the marketplaces, and to be called by men, 'Rabbi, Rabbi.' But you, do not be called 'Rabbi,' for One is your Teacher, the Christ, and you are all brethren. Do not call anyone on earth your father; for One is your Father, He who is

---

[16] J. Oswald Sanders, *Spiritual Leadership*, rev. ed. (Chicago: Moody Press, 1989). p. x.

in heaven. And do not be called teachers; for one is your Teacher, the Christ" (Matt. 23:6-10).[17]

Here is strong evidence that Jesus, while the only rightful King and the only Head of the church, is not entirely opposed to a measure of democracy and egalitarianism in her government and structure. Thus His denunciation of worldly nobility in the church bears some resemblance to the words of Thomas Jefferson in our nation's Declaration of Independence: "All men are created equal." The question, then, is this: If God in heaven is the only undisputed leader of the church, then how can we on earth – as members of that church, His body – best structure and manage ourselves in a way that would please our King?

Some might ask with sincerity if the organization of the church is all that important. Shouldn't we be more concerned with issues such as evangelism, discipleship, and holy living? Indeed we should. But structure and government determine how effectively and freely we are permitted to function as the body of Christ. Ironically, the question of church government thus has everything to do with evangelism, discipleship and holy living. Many Christians seem to think that since we in the church all love God so much, there is no need for a proper structure in order to ensure accountability. A brief review of church history would suggest the contrary. Others confuse theological ignorance with evangelical urgency.

---

[17] Protestant pastors have sometimes implied that because in these verses Jesus forbids calling men "Father," His word of correction here is somehow reserved for a Roman Catholic audience. But He also mentions the titles "Rabbi" and "Teacher," and in other translations, "Leader." His point, clearly, is that no man is due an exalted spiritual status because of his position in the church. Had Jesus felt it necessary to make an exhaustive list of such designations, He doubtless would have included Protestant titles such as "Reverend," "Doctor," and of course, "Pastor."

They argue in effect: "We don't have time to fool with these sorts of silly divisive questions; there's a world dying out there!"

Theologian Howard Snyder nonetheless asks, "Could it be that our structures quench the Spirit?" It's a legitimate question, and as regards authority and leadership, it ventures into largely unexplored theological territory. To make matters worse, the contemporary church – especially in the megachurch model – is often too eager to embrace whatever appears "successful," even if it means sacrificing biblical veracity and spiritual integrity. As Os Guinness notes, this means that in spiritual terms the megachurch is tragically unsuccessful: "Many superchurches are simply artificially inflated local churches with charismatically inflated super-pastors that will not be able to survive their supergrowth."[18] Like Os Guinness, former pastor James Rutz is astounded at how blithely and blindly the church latched on to its own patently unscriptural traditions of exalted leadership:

> The modern concept of the pastor grew out of Wittenberg, Germany, and was but an adaptation of the pastoral duties of a priest!... From that day on, people have written literally millions of books on every theological issue conceivable to the mind of man, yet almost no one has closely questioned the Biblical basis for the all-in-one pastor, a superior being operates as the heart and soul of the church. He is just there.[19]

And because he is "just there," the church is stymied. Sure we want to get involved, but we also want to stand up and be counted, to be seen and be heard. Many of us simply no longer believe it when the pastor rises up to speak on yet another Sunday morning, stands all alone on a raised platform, under a spotlight with a microphone in his hand, looks out over a hushed audience, and tells

---

[18] Guinness, p. 29.

[19] Rutz, p. 69.

us that everyone has an equally vital part to play in the building of the kingdom. Contrary to popular pastoral opinion, the problem is not that we're all too lazy and carnal to get involved. Social analyst George Barna explains:

> Often, pastors complain that there are not enough people willing to be leaders in the church. In actuality...research has shown that there are more than enough people capable and willing to serve in leadership roles... Today, most leadership training programs are carried out via lecture; we tell people *about* leadership, rather than nurture them in the *practice* of leadership. The success stories of leadership development are coming from churches where leadership training is conducted through experience rather than talk.[20]

Barna is onto something. Training must supersede talk. For that to happen, however, an environment must be constructed in which hands-on training can actually take place. This means that old, outworn church structures must be replaced with a new model based on biblical patterns of leadership, fellowship and discipleship. Before the church can ever expect to have revival, it must be reformed. And before it can be reformed it must be decentralized. Jim Peterson concurs, commenting on the loss of the early church practice of "mutual submission between the apostles and elders," a phenomenon never fully recovered in the church – by the reformers or anyone else: "In the centuries immediately following, the freedom of the first century was lost to a hierarchical, controlling structure. This split the church into two castes – clergy and laity – and gave the clergy exclusive control over the ministry."[21]

---

[20] George Barna, *The Frog in the Kettle* (Ventura, CA: Regal Books, 1990), pp. 148-49.

[21] Jim Peterson, *Church without Walls* (Colorado Springs: Navpress, 1992), p. 109.

I believe the time has finally come to tear down the pastoral ivory tower. And I'm not alone. More and more church leaders are coming to the same conclusion. In studying the late twentieth century phenomenon of "new paradigm" churches such as Calvary Chapel, Hope Chapel and the Vineyard, sociologist Donald E. Miller assesses the critical factor of decentralization:

> It directly challenges the legitimacy of a hierarchical structure, as it forcefully raises the question of why another human being should supersede the authority of the relationship between God and the individual.... New paradigm churches believe there is no reason why [authority] should percolate from the top of the organizational hierarchy.... In this regard, the theology of new paradigm groups appears relatively egalitarian, involving lay-persons in ministry, and it invites organizational innovation from the bottom up.[22]

After undergoing many centuries of ineffective and sometimes abusive authoritarian rule, the church in many quarters is just now catching on to the truth of Jesus' words to His zealous but ambitious disciples: "You know that those who are considered rulers over the Gentiles lord it over them, and their great ones exercise authority over them. Yet it shall not be so among you; but whoever desires to be great among you shall be your servant" (Mark 10:42, 43). It appears the church is undergoing a long overdue revolution. But a revolution in the church involves more than simply throwing out old patterns of leadership. It requires a radical reexamination of the church itself.

---

[22] Donald E. Miller, *Reinventing American Protestantism: Christianity in the New Millennium* (Los Angeles: University of California Press, 1997), p. 147.

II. The Church: Repository of Truth

I know he would not be a wolf, but that he sees the Romans are but sheep.

-- Shakespeare, *Julius Caesar*

Of how much more value is a man than a sheep?

-- Matthew 12:12

SCRIPTURE PRESENTS a number of metaphors to describe the church: a physical body, the "body of Christ;" a close-knit family, the "household of God;" and a virgin bride awaiting "the coming of her bridegroom," Jesus Christ. In his first epistle Peter describes the church in glowing terms: "a chosen generation, a holy nation, a royal priesthood, His own special people...the people of God" (1 Pet. 2:9, 10). Yet to hear many preachers, the bride of Christ – the church – is really nothing to write home to Mom about.

Indeed, the church is depicted by some (certainly not all) pastors as basically a bunch of unspiritual, undisciplined, ignorant rebels. To these pastors, the most apt metaphor in Scripture for the church is that of a flock of dirty sheep in desperate need of a shepherd to lead them. Without the pastor to watch over them, these dumb defenseless sheep will eventually get lost in the wilderness, die of hunger or thirst, or be devoured by wolves.

Of course, there is *some* truth to this. Scripture does portray the church as the "flock of God" and Jesus did describe those who believe in Him as sheep who know their master's voice. Moreover, pastors are truly called to aid in the protection of the sheep from a number of spiritual perils. But as with most biblical metaphors, the sheep-shepherd metaphor only takes us so far. It is not a complete picture of how the church should view itself, behave itself, or govern itself. In this case, the analogy breaks down somewhat upon consideration of the pastor as the shepherd – because the pastor also happens to be a sheep. In addressing the shepherd leaders of Israel, the prophet Ezekiel makes it clear that all men are equally "sheepish": "'You are my flock, the flock of My pasture; you are men, and I am the Lord your God,' says the Lord God" (Ezek. 34:31). To those "mighty men of faith and power" who have never realized the truth of this: Welcome to the flock!

In much the same way that a false teacher is a wolf in sheep's clothing, a pastor is a sheep in shepherd's clothing. In other words a pastor fulfills a role of ministry given him by God and not of himself. In fact, the Bible indicates that many times the sheep go astray not because of their own sin, but because of the selfishness of their shepherds. God pointedly accused the leaders of Ezekiel's day of just that:

> You eat the fat and clothe yourselves with the wool; you slaughter the fatlings, but you do not feed the flock. The weak you have not strengthened, nor have you healed those who were sick, nor bound up the broken, nor brought back what was driven away, nor sought what was lost; but with force and cruelty you have ruled them. So they were scattered because there was no shepherd ... (Ezek. 34: 3-5).

I mention all this because the sheep metaphor often finds its way into matters of church government, and is used to justify a condescending refusal on the part of leaders to allow the church body to share in important decisions regarding her own purpose and destiny After all, we sheep are simply too *dumb* to know what to do. [In many cases we *are* a bit short on understanding, but the extension of this belief into all matters precludes the growth of the believers in wisdom and knowledge of the Scriptures, which are "able to make you wise" (2 Tim. 3:15).]

To whatever extent the church is ignorant of God's truth, she is missing what is clearly the will of God as revealed in His Word: "I do not want you to be ignorant," declared Paul to the Corinthians (1 Cor. 12:1). Unlike Paul, too many pastors see ignorance on the part of the church as something of a virtue, in that it leads to a dependence upon leadership for the answers. Hans Küng is a Catholic theologian, but his arguments for laity involvement in the decision-making process of the church apply just as well to the typical Protestant assembly (excepting a few of the congregational variety):

> It is precisely here that the question of the status of the laity in the church arises in the most practical way. For as long as I can contribute advice and work, but am excluded from decision-making, I remain, no matter how many fine things are said about my status, a second class member of this community.[23]

There is in many churches a tendency to disregard the substance of a man's claims because of his presumed spiritual status as a sheep, a mere "layman." I can appreciate the words of Glenn Wagner, commenting on a wave of teaching in the church known as the "shepherding movement":

> This movement failed largely because it took a metaphor and turned it into a literal truth. Yes, the Bible sometimes calls us sheep, but that doesn't mean we are like sheep in every respect. We don't walk on four legs. We don't graze on hills or grow wool.[24]

He concludes: "To take the metaphor beyond the Bible's clearly intended meaning often leads to serious abuses." The church is not

---

[23] Hans Küng, *Reforming the Church Today* (New York: Crossroad Publishing, 1990), p. 75.

[24] Glenn E. Wagner, *Escape from Church, Inc.* (Grand Rapids: Zondervan, 1999), p. 129.

a bunch of ignorant sheep led by an all-knowing pastor. Neither is the church an army of soldiers under the command of a church version of General Patton. It is remarkable how often leaders refer to the church as an "army," when the term is not once used in the New Testament to describe an assembly of believers. Nor is the church a kingdom. Granted, the church is the visible expression of the kingdom of God on the earth, Bonhoeffer's "visible community," what Jesus termed "a city on a hill." But at the same time the kingdom extends far beyond the relatively small visions and miniscule efforts of individual believers, churches, pastors and denominations. Vineyard founder John Wimber makes this point in his little book, *Kingdom Fellowship*: "The early disciples preached the kingdom, not the church.... Not once did Jesus equate the disciples with the kingdom. This means that though the church is integral to the kingdom of God, it isn't the kingdom itself."[25]

All the same, great numbers of leaders still refer to the local church in monarchical and military language. Charles Colson has written an excellent book entitled *The Body*, yet in it he describes the church in terms of military organization:

> Its recruitment is universal, but it has to be broken down   into individual fighting units. It may have command structures, such as denominations or episcopal government.... These are visible structures we create to enable God's army – the Body – to do the job it is called to do.[26]

I find it ironic that in the context of structure Colson should refer to the church as a dualism, "God's army – the Body," for in structural terms it cannot possibly be both. Paul argued that "those members

---

[25] John Wimber, *Kingdom Fellowship: Living Together as the Body of Christ* (Ann Arbor, MI: Servant, 1989), p. 15.

[26] Charles Colson, *The Body: Being Light in Darkness* (Dallas: Word Publishing, 1992), p. 69.

of the body which we think to be less honorable, on these we bestow greater honor…" (1 Cor. 12:23). Yet I rather doubt that a five-star general, bedecked with medals and ribbons, and attended by any number of cowering subordinates, would encourage honoring some unheard-of private out on the field of battle *above* himself.

In the New Testament, no man has a higher measure of delegated authority than the apostle Paul. By the authority vested in him via a harrowing personal encounter with Christ Himself, Paul reserved the right to correct and chasten a great number of well-established churches, however and whenever he should come and visit: "But I will come to you shortly, if the Lord wills, and I will know, not the word of those who are puffed up, but the power. For the kingdom of God is not in word but in power. What do you want? Shall I come to you with a rod, or in love and a spirit of gentleness?" (I Cor. 4:19-21)

If anyone should be expected to brandish his authority and show contempt for the lesser, common souls comprising the church, it would be the apostle Paul. Nowhere in Scripture does Paul do anything like this. In his only really in-depth discussion of "who's who" in the church in terms of status, he likens the church not to an army but to a body, in which all the parts are equally vital, no matter their prominence or visibility. In the process he openly repudiates authoritarianism: "And those members of the body which we think to be less honorable, on these we bestow greater honor" (1 Cor. 12: 3).

Rather than regard the church with disgust, contempt, or suspicion, Paul refers to her as a repository of truth in the earth – "the pillar and ground of the truth." He understood that the church in truth consists of saved, spiritual people, who are destined to one day judge matters of eternal import. In his letters to the churches, Paul to my knowledge never mentions a pastor or a leader – though on occasion he makes reference to the "bishops and deacons" as part of his intended audience. Some would argue that the reason for this is simply that Paul *was* the pastor of these churches. If that is true (it is *not* true, we will see), it only strengthens my case: Since

Paul could not possibly have led all the churches at once, the local church in the first century obviously had the wherewithal to function without constant pastoral supervision.

Paul's first letter to the Corinthians, for instance, is addressed simply "to the church of God in Corinth." Yet in this letter to the church are guidelines for dealing with a pronounced problem of sexual immorality in the congregation. Though this is a spiritual crisis of the highest order, Paul doesn't even bother to come in person to straighten out the mess. Instead, he merely alerts the church to the importance of the issue, and then trusts the church to handle it. (And according to Second Corinthians, they handled it just fine, apparently by taking a vote on the matter: "This punishment that was inflicted by the majority is sufficient for such a man" - 2 Cor. 2:6.) The apostle also entrusted the church body to identify and put under discipline the disobedient and the divisive, as well as judge matters of ongoing conflict within the church (2 Thess. 3:14; Rom. 16:17; 1 Cor. 6:1).

In her collective wisdom, the church is the highest and purest institution on earth. Because of this the church retains in Scripture – at least in certain situations – a higher authority than its pastors or leaders. This is no clearer than in matters of conflict between brethren. In Matthew's Gospel, Jesus warned of the inevitable: "Offenses must come." No matter how spiritual the church, no matter how noble its leaders, not matter how wonderful its people, the church would experience its share of offenses. He then offered some explicit instructions on how to deal with such situations:

> "Moreover, if your brother sins against you, go and tell him his fault between you and him alone. If he hears you, you have gained your brother. But if he will not hear, take with you one or two more, that 'by the mouth of two or three witnesses every word may be established.' And if he refuses to hear them, tell it to the church. And if he refuses to hear even the church, let him be to you like a heathen and a tax collector" (Matt. 18: 15-17).

34

Jesus here gives a lesson in ecclesiastical jurisprudence, and lays out the procedure in sequence. In a personal conflict, He says, first tell the matter to the offending party alone. Hopefully, h'll listen and that will be that. If he doesn't listen, step two is to bring along some Christian friends who are familiar with the situation as mediators in the conflict. If he still won't listen, Jesus says to "tell it to the church." At that point, if he refuses "even to hear the church," then he is to be regarded as an unsaved, unspiritual individual.

Curiously, the highest level of appeal in this process is not the office of some infallibly anointed pastor or leader, but that collective body of believers known as the church. Jesus apparently sees something in the church other than fat and wool. He sees in her the ability to discern a spiritual matter and render a just verdict. Paul implied much the same in his exhortation to the Corinthians, to judge their own disputes: "Dare any of you, having a matter against another, go to law before the unrighteous and not before the saints? Do you not know that the saints will judge the world?" (1 Cor. 6:1, 2) Like a great number of believers today, the Corinthian Christians were unaware of their considerable stature in Christ.

At this point it might be fair to ask: *Why, then, is the church today so weak, ineffective, and compromised?* Part of the answer, at least, is that leadership has so dominated the flow of ministry that the church is stunted. It might be growing numerically, but certainly not in terms of congregational maturity. A former pastor with the Assemblies of God, Melvin Hodges has pinpointed the problem in the context of overseas missions:

> As missionaries, we have too often trained the converts in dependence upon *us*, rather than in *responsibility*. It may be because we have an overprotectiveness for our converts; it may be that unconsciously we desire to be the head and have people look to us as the indispensable man; it may stem from our lack of faith in the Holy Spirit to do His work in maturing the converts. But for whatever reason, the fact remains that

remains that weak churches are often the product of the missionaries' wrong approach to their task.[27]

Hodges argues at length that the church has been granted by God the wisdom and authority of localized self-government. A true New Testament church is *indigenous* – that is, self-governing. God is attempting to train the entire church, and not merely an elite class of shepherds, to more effectively minister the gospel in the earth. Indeed, this is the essential calling of leaders in the church, "for the equipping of the saints for the work of the ministry" (Eph. 4:11, 12). Leadership ministry is characterized by sharing (not hoarding) the wealth of spiritual knowledge and experience with all believers, so that they may one day minister just as well. This means that the pastor may have to relinquish his spotlight for a time, in order to train others to share his place behind the pulpit. To surmount the tendency of leaders to single-handedly rule the church will require some radical reorganization. As it stands now, the destiny of most churches rests precariously on the shoulders of one individual:

> The fact is, most ministries and many churches depend on the genius and/or expertise of the key leader for their success. The potential effectiveness and scope of this ministry is thereby limited to what the key leader can do by himself or herself, or can directly supervise. If on the way to work one morning a cement truck buries the ministry leader under ten tons of quick-dry cement, you might as well bury the ministry too.[28]

---

[27] Melvin L. Hodges, *The Indigenous Church* (Springfield, MO: Gospel Publishing House, 1953), p. 17.

[28] Robert E. Logan and Larry Short, *Mobilizing for Compassion* (Grand Rapids: Fleming H. Revell, 1994), pp. 155-156.

Viola and Barna express the same thought with equal bluntness: "Remove the pastor, and Protestantism as we know it would die."[29] When it comes to leadership in the local church, then, two (or more) heads are better than one. This is exactly the mandate for pastoral leadership in the New Testament, and the subject of the next chapter.

---

[29] Viola & Barna, p. 106.

III. Elders: Overseers of the Flock

Setting aside every other business, the guardians will dedicate themselves wholly to the maintenance of freedom in the state, making this their craft...

-- Plato, *The Republic*

The elders who are among you I exhort.... Shepherd the flock of God which is among you, serving as overseers, not by compulsion but willingly, not for dishonest gain but eagerly; nor as being lords over those entrusted to you, but being examples to the flock.

-- 1 Peter 5:1-3

MANY OF US can still recall the stunning series of financial excesses and moral failures committed by prominent church leaders – Jim Bakker, Jimmy Swaggart, Oral Roberts, Robert Tilton, etc. – beginning in the mid-eighties. Christian leaders have theorized for the last few decades on the causes of "Pearlygate," usually listing personal sins such as pride, unbelief, sensual lust, and the love of money. Consequently they propose solutions, such as prayer and repentance, that are generally wise and commendable, but in this instance a bit short-sighted.

Addressing the problem in *The Integrity Crisis*, Warren Wiersbe means well but almost undoubtedly oversimplifies when he says, "The answer is – revival."[30] Few church leaders to my

---

[30] Warren Wiersbe, *The Integrity Crisis* (Nashville: Oliver Nelson, 1988), p. 119.

knowledge have seriously suggested that church structure could be a contributing factor to this troubling trend. Yet the often extreme reverence offered up to modern pastors almost certainly plays a part in their growing tendency to fail.

Preachers for centuries have expounded on the sin of King David in committing adultery with Bathsheba, for instance, strictly in terms of personal failure. He is blamed for staying home instead of doing battle, looking at a nude woman when he should have looked away, ignoring a warning from one of his servants, and finally, inviting the woman over to do the deed. Likewise, Bathsheba is blamed for bathing outdoors and complying with the king's wishes. I suppose these points are valid. But can anyone really expect a king to resist temptation, listen to his servants, or respect the husband of a married woman when he is under no obligation from his peers to do so? And how can anyone expect Bathsheba – foolish as she may have been – to defy the express order of her king?

The fact is that power makes for excess. A man who senses no accountability to others is destined to experience unusually powerful temptations. Though an advocate of traditional leadership structures, Charles Colson calls the exalted view of pastoral leadership in modern churches the "pedestal complex." This he sees as the greatest source of temptation in the ministry: "The strong leader who builds a large and successful church is often not held to account... For this reason, more and more pastors seem to be falling..."[31] Charles Kraft echoes Colson's concerns:

> It is unfortunate that our worldview assumptions lead us to believe that those in positions of ministry are spiritually strong enough to be independent.... Many of the Christian leaders who have recently fallen from high positions might still be effective for Christ if they had been accountable to someone.[32]

---

[31] Colson, p. 299.

[32] Charles H. Kraft, *Christianity with Power* (Ann Arbor, MI:

Like most Christians, Colson and Kraft offer no real solution in the way of pastoral accountability, except to advise pastors to find a "mentor" whom they can "go to" in time of temptation or failure. But this version of accountability is based on the willingness of the pastor to report to his good friend (and the willingness of his good friend to correct him) precisely when he would rather not; i.e., it is not real accountability at all. Hence, the structure of the church ensures that the problem of nagging temptation remains. Giving a sinful man beset with temptations – pastor though he may be – sovereign charge of a congregation is like leaving an ex-convict with a long rap sheet all alone in charge of the company vault. Eventually, he is likely to fail.

Pastoral transgressions are not limited, however, to sexual sin and financial fraud. Church leaders ruling absolutely over a church often feel free to intimidate, manipulate, deceive, insult and otherwise abuse the church. Ronald Enroth has compiled a large body of evidence in *Churches That Abuse* demonstrating that emotional and psychological abuse in the church is not a mere aberration: "[T]here is abundant evidence that a serious problem of abuse exists in the Christian community." However, because the church has been carved up, like Bosnia and Herzegovina, into over 2,000 independent groupings, the problem will not be going away any time soon:

> But what about rescuing the leaders and salvaging the followers? That is a major challenge facing the conventional evangelical church. Most of the abusive churches I have studied are independent, autonomous groups. They are not part of a denomination or network that could provide checks and balances or any kind of accountability.[33]

Servant, 1989), p. 175.

[33] Ronald Enroth, *Churches That Abuse* (Grand Rapids: Zondervan, 1992), p. 235.

This obvious need for accountability in the church is what first led me to question the biblical validity of conventional church structures. But even then I had not really questioned the standard arrangement around the pastoral office. In my original outline for this little book, in fact, the third chapter was entitled, "The Pastor: Overseer of the Flock." My understanding of New Testament church government was that the congregation consists of a pastor, the shepherd of the flock, and under him a council of elders or deacons, and then the entire church body. This pattern of leadership has been followed almost without exception for the last 1800 years, regardless of denomination or doctrine. It is therefore a very strong tradition. My view, revised through recent study, is that this is a false, unhealthy, and unbiblical tradition. Perhaps it is because He knows human nature that God nowhere appoints hierarchical leadership in the New Testament church.

I have chosen instead to dedicate this chapter to the function of the *elders* (plural) for reasons to follow. To begin, the word "pastor(s)" appears once, and only once, in the New Testament: "And He Himself gave some to be...pastors" (Eph. 4:11). *Vine's Dictionary* comments on this word, *poimēn*: "Pastors guide as well as feed the flock.; cf. Acts 20:28, which, with v.17, indicates that this was the service committed to elders (overseers or bishops)...."[34] That is, *pastor* is more a function than an office, a function which belongs to a group of leaders known as *elders*, or bishops. This may come as a surprise to some. To others it may seem merely a question of semantics, as the church today simply refers to its elders as pastors.

But to further confound matters, Paul in his so-called pastoral epistles instructs a young apostle named Titus to "appoint elders" – rather than "hire a pastor" – "in every city" to lead the churches (Titus 1:5). Moreover, in his general epistles Paul at no time ad-

---

[34] W.E. Vine, *Vine's Expository Dictionary of New Testament Words* (Nashville: Thomas Nelson, 1985), p. 462.

dresses a single presiding pastor or bishop, but instead writes to "all who are in Rome, called as saints;" "the church of God which is in Corinth;" "the churches of Galatia;" "the saints who are in Ephesus;" "the saints and the faithful ministers who in Christ who are in Collosse;" and "the church of the Thessalonians." Only to the Philippians does he mention local leaders, after first greeting the church at large, and then in plural: "the saints in Christ Jesus who are in Philippi, with the bishops and deacons."

What this suggests is a plurality of leadership in the local church that is completely contrary to the overly simplified (and overly autocratic) pattern of clergy and laity. This may sound radical, but only because we in the church have completely abandoned the New Testament pattern for so long. Despite a wealth of evidence suggesting that the contemporary church has become literally dysfunctional, it continues with the same ineffective, unscriptural framework. In his analysis of the function of the elder in the first century church, Philip Greenslade reveals a rarely mentioned aspect of New Testament leadership:

> He is not...an autocratic manager of the people. Nor is he a representative or delegate of some sectional interest in the church. He is *with others* a guardian, an overseer, a shepherd of the whole flock, who watches over the sheep, succours the weak and is alert to what threatens them.... The elder in short is a man who exercises a clear pastoral ministry [emphasis added].[35]

Pastoral ministry in the New Testament church belongs to a group of leaders known as the *elders,* elsewhere termed *bishops*. I'm not sure why this pattern has been so persistently denied in the typical church, except that the church has a long-standing – traditional – love of tradition. But leadership by a group (how large?) of elders

---

[35] Philip Greenslade, *Leadership, Greatness, and Servanthood* (Minneapolis: Bethany House, 1985), p. 186.

is the biblical model. This is a fact acknowledged by virtually all commentators, but ignored by most pastors. Charles C. Ryrie outlines the place of elders as follows:

> Without doubt elders were the principal leaders of New Testament churches. Though all do not agree, it appears that elders and bishops occupied the same position in the church – the term elder emphasizing more the office and the term bishop emphasizing more the function of that office, namely general oversight... The question of how many elders there were in each assembly is debated. Clearly there were several elders in each city where there were churches.[36]

That the church today for the most part has neglected the role of the elders perhaps explains the modern office of the assistant pastor, who in the New Testament did not exist. He must exist in the typical contemporary church, because the pastor – no matter his gifting, his heart or his motives – simply cannot carry out all the duties required of him. Since the "deacons" are available to complete delegated tasks, but are not allowed to share in leadership decisions, the stress and strain of singular leadership becomes too great and the pastor is compelled to hire from outside what is in essence a "backup shepherd" to share his duties.

If the biblical pattern is valid, however, the pastor has access to a pool of qualified candidates right under his nose – in his own congregation. By the time his responsibilities become too much to manage, he should have at hand a good number of men equipped to help bear the burden. Striking in its contrast with modern churches is this sharing of burdens – even leadership burdens – by a number of capable, albeit "officially" unrecognized leaders. Vine again describes these elders as

---

[36] Charles C. Ryrie, *A Survey of Bible Doctrine* (Chicago: Moody Press, 1972), p. 143.

those who, being raised up and qualified by the work of the Holy Spirit, were appointed to have the spiritual care of, and to exercise the oversight over, the churches.... The divine arrangement seen throughout the NT was for a plurality of these to be appointed in each church, Acts 14:23; 20:17; Phili. 1:1; 1 Tim. 5:17; Titus 1:5.[37]

Acts 20 is most instructive. Here is the only instance in which Paul refers to the leaders as shepherds, yet his audience is not a group of pastors from various congregations, but a group of elders from a single congregation, the church at Ephesus. The elders actually constitute a joint pastorate. David A. Mappes concurs: "One important observation is that those who labor in preaching and teaching are plural. There are several teaching elders, not just one."[38]

A study of early church history reveals the same form. Historian David F. Wright notes that leadership in the first century church was largely a matter of teamwork: "Congregational life was directed by a team or group, commonly known as 'presbyters' – that is, elders or fathers in the faith – or 'bishops." He concludes, "There was no counterpart to 'the minister' of today in earliest Christianity."[39] In defining the eldership for the conventional church, Dick Iverson draws attention to the beauty of teamwork thriving amid diversity: "Who are the elders? They are the overseers, the parents of the church. Do they have various functions?

---

[37] Vine, p. 195.

[38] Zuck, p. 88.

[39] David F. Wright, "Early Christian Beliefs," from Tim Dowley, ed., *Eerdman's Handbook to the History of Christianity* (Grand Rapids: Eerdman's, 1977).

Yes, according to Scripture… They are to govern the church, however, only as a team."[40]

My only question is: Where are these elders today? All I can see in most churches is a pastor, a congregation, and a group of men who may be designated "elders" or "deacons" or "the council" or some such, but who do not, and cannot, share with the pastor the responsibilities of instructing, teaching, counseling, and otherwise leading (serving) the flock. In many churches, they are in place strictly to support the pastoral agenda (which of course is to be unquestionably interpreted as God's agenda). The benefits which would be reaped by implementing the New Testament pattern of shared leadership – and its implied shared accountability – would be enormous. A biblical structure could thus prevent the sort of burnout that currently plagues the church: "The most pervasive ministry frustration expressed by pastors is that they feel they bear the burden of ministry alone. Relatively few pastors feel as if they are part of a team …"[41]

Despite the fact that the appointment of an eldership to the church would clearly be wise, encouraging, resourceful and helpful, many will doubtless object to this setup as leadership by a mere committee. I can only answer that the appointment of a group of elders – or pastors, or bishops, the titles don't matter – in the church is biblical. Others would argue that the eldership does not in fact exist, that the plurality of leaders is an unwarranted interpretation of New Testament texts. The *Wycliffe Bible Commentary*, for instance, offers these remarks on Acts 14:23: "The language suggests that there were several elders in each local church; but the church in a given city may have consisted in a number of house

---

[40] C. Peter Wagner, ed., *The New Apostolic Churches* (Ventura, CA: Regal Books, 1998), p. 173. Note that while I do not endorse every aspect of Wagner's theology, I have found his analysis of leadership insightful from a structural perspective.

[41] Barna, p. 139.

congregations with an elder ruling over each group."[42] This argument fails to account for the fact that even the house group was referred to as a church. Consider Paul's greetings to Philemon and his companions: "To Philemon our beloved friend and fellow laborer, to the beloved Apphia, Archippus our fellow soldier, and to the church in your house" (Philemon 1:1, 2). Now if the biblical mandate is the appointment of "elders in every church" (Acts 14:23), and even the house group is in fact a church, then there is little justification for assuming that there was but a single elder in each of the early church congregations.

Others still have argued that the reference to the qualifications of a "bishop" (singular) as opposed to "deacons" (plural) in 1 Timothy 3 implies that there was only one bishop in each congregation. Not only is this supposition contrary to the rest of the New Testament, but is inconsistent with the calling of deacons. Since Paul describes the office of the bishop again in Titus, but there makes no reference to the deacons, does this mean that he had changed his mind and there were no deacons to be appointed in the churches after all?

It seems safe to say that Paul's emphasis in his listing of qualifications was on the nature of spiritual ministry, regardless of how many ministers there may be: "A bishop must be blameless." This is another way of saying that blamelessness is required of *bishops* collectively. Pastors often cite Hebrews 13:7 and 13:17 to bolster their authority, but even these verses refer to leadership in the plural: "those who have the rule over you." If the pastor is the only one who has the rule, and everyone in the church has but one pastor, who are these other leaders over the church? It's really no mystery. They are the elders. Viola and Barna add, "Among the flock were the elders (shepherds or overseers). These men all had equal standing. There was no hierarchy among them."[43]

---

[42] Charles F. Pfeiffer, ed., *The Wycliffe Bible Commentary* (Chicago: Moody Press, 1962), p. 1150.

[43] Viola & Barna, p. 110.

In Scripture the elders are a localized group of leaders who "labor in the word and doctrine," "shepherd the flock of God," and "support the weak." As a council united in purpose, they effectively minister to the church. To anyone suffering from sickness in the early church, James advised, "Let him call for the elders [plural] of the church [singular], and let them pray over him" (James 5:14). It would be difficult to imagine, as the singular bishop-pastor-overseer theory requires, that a sick man in the first century would really be expected to travel from church to church throughout the region, gathering together all the pastors so that they could at last pray for his ever-worsening condition. It makes more sense to assume that the elders referenced by James worked within the same local congregation.

What such a pluralized leadership structure implies is that local church government depends on fellowship rather than fear, on cooperation rather than coercion. In fact, without love and fellowship among the appointed elders, the New Testament pattern is doomed to failure. On the other hand, if leadership functions on any other principle *but* love and fellowship, it is bound to fail anyway – regardless of structure.

In the hierarchical-military model leadership can function without any love at all. The eldership, on the other hand, by its very nature hinges upon the wisdom of consensus and the power of genuine fellowship. I leave the last word of this chapter to Ray Stedman, who once remarked on the concept of a body of elders as central to the godly oversight of the church:

> The task of elders is not to run the church themselves, but to determine how the Lord wishes to run the church…. In the day-to-day church decisions, elders are to find the mind of the Lord through an uncoerced unanimity, reached after thorough biblical discussion…. The point is, no one man is the sole ex-

pression of the mind of the Spirit; no one individual has the authority from God to direct the church.[44]

---

[44] Ray Stedman, "Should the Pastor Play Pope?", *Moody Monthly* (July-August 1976), p. 42.

IV. Deacons: Ministers to the Poor

Middle managers are to be autonomous – but no longer as rule interpreters of "functional integrity" in the traditional... organizational structure. Instead, middle managers are to be responsible for seeking out and battering down the very functional barriers that they were formerly paid to protect.

-- Tom Peters, *Thriving on Chaos*

For those who have served well as deacons obtain for themselves a good standing and great boldness in the faith which is in Christ Jesus.

-- 1 Timothy 3:13

THE BOOK OF ACTS is a marvelous record of church expansion. It begins with an explosion of growth, as Peter in the second chapter preaches on the streets and an astounding three thousand souls are added to the church in a day. From there, increase is steady: "And the Lord added to the church daily those who were being saved" (Acts 2:47). A short time later, the number of believers is listed at "about five thousand" (4:4). Besides phenomenal growth, the disciples in Acts experienced supernatural visitations in the form of Holy Spirit baptisms, physical healings, even a divine jailbreak. These men of God were on the cutting edge of a great move of God.

In the midst of all this was a problem: "Now in those days, when the number of the disciples was multiplying, there arose a complaint against the Hebrews by the Hellenists, because their widows were neglected in the daily distribution" (Acts 6:1). This was a volatile social situation, one for which the apostles had not the time to address or correct. Instead, they addressed the church: "Then the twelve summoned the multitude of the disciples and said, 'It is not desirable that we should leave the word of God and serve tables. Therefore, brethren, seek out from among you seven men of good reputation, full of the Holy Spirit and wisdom, whom we may appoint over this business" (v. 2, 3).

In the context of church government, it is worth noting that the apostles did not choose the first deacons themselves, but left the decision for the church to make. So the church chose the seven, who were appointed specifically to minister to these poor widows. While the text does not designate these men as deacons, it does provide a job description which fits that given deacons in the New Testament. As Eric L. Titus notes in *The Interpreter's Commentary*:

> Acts 6:1-6 relates the appointment of 7 deacons who would relieve the apostles of the necessity to "serve tables" and would care for the needs of widows of the Hellenists.... Here the close connection of deacons with bishops and the similarity of qualifications suggests the importance of the office.[45]

Very clearly, these deacons were chosen to serve the practical needs of the church. "Deacon" is translated from *diakonos* in Greek, which means simply, *servant*. The deacon's job description is very similar to the elder's or pastor's. In fact, it is so similar to it that there is some confusion as to where exactly the pastoral ministry leaves off and that of the deacons picks up.

While attending an assembly known as Cielo Vista Church some years ago in El Paso, Texas, I received a letter from one of the deacons. After introducing himself to me by name and then as "your deacon," he described his responsibilities to the congregation

---

[45] Charles M. Laymon, ed., *The Interpreter's One-Volume Commentary on the Bible* (Nashville: Abingdon, 1971), p. 886.

and in the process gave a good working definition of the deacon's ministry:

> Because of the growing size of the congregation, the church membership has been divided into small "deacon families" so you can get to know people in a smaller group and have someone to call if you need help or encouragement. Being a deacon is a church function, not an elected office....

In the aforementioned situation of Acts 6, the deacons serve to mediate the resentment and hostility that had developed between a certain ethnic group and the apostles, who were essentially accused of favoring others above them. The deacons step in to resolve the conflict by actively serving the present needs. Deacons are mentioned by name – that is, translated "deacons" – in only two chapters of the New Testament: Philippians 1, and 1 Timothy 3. Thus, I will not pretend to know more about them than what Scripture and early church history attests.

However, the prevalence of the Greek word *diákonos* throughout the Gospels and the letters of Paul indicates that the deacons' essential function – to serve and minister to the spiritually and financially impoverished – is inseparable from service to Christ Himself. Jesus in fact uses the same word to refer to Christians in general, those who "serve" God in faith (John 12:26). Paul used it of himself, as (with Apollos) "ministers through whom you believed" (1 Cor. 3:5); and "a minister according to the gift of the grace of God given to me" (Eph. 3:7) – among other places in the epistles. The *Oxford Dictionary of the Bible* adds to the richness of the term, and hence of the ministry:

> The deacons in the Church are to embody personal integrity and their role is that of a scribe, whereas the task of teaching is entrusted to the presbyter.... From Rom. 16:1, where Phoebe is mentioned, it would seem that the NT women could be regarded as deacons.... The functions of the [deacons] were

administrative and liturgical in the early church, but they were not inferior officers.[46]

Again, the interchangeability of terminology, function and office among these early church leaders attests to the informality of the church's structure. In a sense, Paul was as much a "deacon" as Philip or Stephen. On the other hand, there were men in each congregation officially ordained as "deacons" by the whole assembly. "Qualifications given in 1 Timothy 3 show that deacons were not considered ordinary lay members of the church."[47]

So here is a group of men with overlapping functions (some were evangelists for example) but who were nonetheless somehow distinct from the congregation – while of course a part of it. They apparently serve as a structural buffer or cushion between two parties with the potential to become factions – the elders and the general congregation. Deacons are equally at ease with both leaders and led, and thus help to obliterate the occasionally and unnecessarily sharp divisions between the two.

The picture that continually emerges from this study of the early church is of a leadership structure marked not by rigid authoritarianism but by flexibility, shared responsibilities, and mutual respect and cooperation. Whereas the elders are appointed by the apostles, the deacons are chosen by the church. The channels of authority therefore flow "from the top down," but also "from the bottom up" – with the deacons meeting the elders somewhere in the middle.

---

[46] W.R.F. Browning, *The Oxford Dictionary of the Bible* (New York: Oxford, 1996), p. 93.

[47] J.D. Douglas and Merrill C. Tenney, *The NIV Compact Dictionary of the Bible* (Grand Rapids: Zondervan, 1989), p. 149.

V. Apostles: Pioneers in the Harvest

Wesley must have failed, had he not possessed unlimited energy, a genius for administration, and the power to impose his will on the vast scattered organization. He built up his organization on autocratic lines. He was never a democrat and never pretended to be a democrat, and in this he resembled the founders of all great religious movements.

-- Arnold Lunn, *John Wesley*

Am I not an apostle? Am I not free? Have I not seen Christ Jesus our Lord? If I am not an apostle to others, yet doubtless I am to you. For you are the seal of my apostleship in the Lord.

-- 1 Corinthians 9:1-2

FOR ALL THOSE "Attila the Hun" types who are disinterested, disbelieving, or just plain disgusted with all this talk about love and collaboration in leadership, there is still a calling in the kingdom of God (and a chapter in this book) just for you. God has reserved a special place in the church for the hard-boiled, insensitive, abrasive, aggressive, no-nonsense types so often associated with leadership. They are the apostles: diligent, disciplined warriors of the kingdom who enjoy a challenge almost as much as they despise the status quo. (I'm probably not being fair. The apostles, Paul, Peter, and John all spoke a great deal of love. Still, in light of their rugged personalities as depicted in Scripture, it would be fair to say that it took much learning and experience before they could state with honesty, "But we were gentle among you, just as a nursing mother cherishes her own children" – 1 Thess. 2:7).

But the apostleship is not simply an office created by God so that his church could include samples from all human temperaments. Apostles are prominent, visible leaders. They lead from the front, because that's exactly where they belong. They have heard directly from God, on occasion have met with God, and have been called by God to an arduous task. Their role is vital in the church because they wield authority given from Christ himself. Apostles retain in Christ the authority to correct, rebuke, chasten and challenge a congregation to new heights. The apostle has the spiritual clout to put an end to petty squabbles and political infighting – even among the elders.

It may sound like heresy, but apostles gain much of their authority the old fashioned way (they *earn* it). In the New Testament churches, apostles are the pioneers. They start churches from nothing, in cities and regions where no one ever thought to start a church before. Paul described the essence of apostleship in 1 Corinthians 3: "As a wise master builder I have laid the foundation, and another builds on it" (v. 10). Paul actually avoided the way of easy success, preferring to stake out new ground. "And so I have made it my aim.to preach the gospel, not where Christ was named, lest I should build on another man's foundation" (Rom. 15:20).

John Eckhardt likens the apostle to a spiritual entrepreneur, one who essentially "pioneers" in all that he does: "The apostle is first and foremost a pioneer. Apostles are the first to go into a new territory or the first to present a new truth." He draws the practical conclusion: "We cannot take old models to this generation and expect to reach them."[48] This building, pioneering ministry is the basis of the apostle's authority, which separates him from the countless preachers and teachers claiming to have a word from God: "For though you might have ten thousand instructors in Christ, yet you do not have many fathers; for in Christ Jesus I have begotten you through the gospel" (1 Cor. 4:15). As a true apostle, Paul bore no resemblance to the professional pastors of today, who

---

[48] Cited in C. P. Wagner, p. 49.

take over churches and establish growth not by conversion but by transfer (from other churches).

Apostles in the New Testament aren't merely hard workers; they are soldiers who have paid a heavy price for their ministry. Whereas "trials" in the modern church consist typically of flat tires, headaches, and problems with coworkers, in the early church the apostles paid for their ministry with physical loss and physical pain. Paul appeals to his personal "scars and stripes" as another legitimate basis of spiritual authority:

> Are they ministers of Christ? – I speak as a fool – I am more: in labors more abundant, in stripes above measure, in prisons more frequently, in deaths often. From the Jews five times I received forty stripes minus one. Three times I was beaten with rods; once I was stoned; three times I was shipwrecked; a night and a day I have been in the deep; in journeys often, in perils of waters, in perils from robbers, in perils of my own countrymen, in perils of the Gentiles, in perils in the city, in perils in the wilderness, in perils in the sea, in perils among false brethren; in weariness and toil, in sleeplessness often, in hunger and thirst, in fastings often, in cold and nakedness – beside the other things, what comes upon my daily: my deep concern for all the churches (2 Cor. 11:23-28).

The apostle's office is critical. Among ministers in the church, only he can provide the kind of strong leadership that can virtually *force* – by force of character and a godly anointing – changes to take place. Apostles are called by God to plant and oversee entire church networks, and are therefore not voted in or out of office. As J. C. Beker discloses in reference to Paul, theirs is consequently a unique and powerful ministry:

> Paul is extremely self-conscious about his apostolate. He has an acute sense of authority and of territorial rights over his mission field.... Texts like 1 Cor. 4:15 and 2 Cor. 10:13-18 demonstrate that Paul exercised his "father right" over his

churches as a claim to absolute authority. Moreover, he identifies his own message with the truth of the gospel in Gal. 1:7-10 and utters an eschatological curse on those who disagree with his gospel.[49]

Given these extreme assertions of authority, it should be emphasized that Paul spoke in terms of fatherhood and even something like ownership because he literally poured out his blood, sweat and tears to found those churches and converts in the faith. Small wonder that he defended those churches against profiteering false teachers and legalistic oppressors with such rabid tenacity!

I believe the apostolic ministry is still a valid form of church leadership in the twenty-first century: "And He Himself gave some to be apostles..." (Eph. 4:11). Of course, the question debated by theologians is not whether there were ever apostles in the church but whether they should still be hanging around over two thousand years later. Ephesians gives the answer, indicating that apostles (along with prophets, evangelists, and other leaders) would continue to be risen up "till we all come to the unity of the faith and of the knowledge of the Son of God..." (v. 13). Given that the church has not yet attained such an ideal state of unity and knowledge, it follows that the apostolic ministry is still valid.

In fact, apostles supply the leadership authority that would otherwise be woefully wanting in the church structure reviewed thus far. Whereas churches are accountable to elders, and elders to churches, and deacons to both, the apostles – though in Scripture willingly accountable to all others in the church – retain authority over most aspects of life in the church. When lies and chaos threaten the peace and sanctity of the church, apostles set things in order and get the people of God back on track.

In *Church without Walls* Jim Peterson reinstates the relevancy of the "fivefold ministry" of Ephesians 4, beginning with the apos-

---

[49] J. Christiaan Beker, *Paul the Apostle: The Triumph of God in Life and Thought* (Philadelphia: Fortress, p. 1980), p. 4.

tolic calling and office: "It took the full spectrum of these functions... for God's people to fulfill their mission to the first-century generation. It requires the same today."[50] Reflecting on the gradual development of his own apostolic ministry out of more traditional structures, John Eckhardt drew an almost identical conclusion: "It takes all five of these ministry gifts operating in the church to properly mature God's people for the work of the ministry. When the apostle is absent, the saints will lack the apostolic character they need to fulfill the Great Commission."[51] Nowhere does Scripture even hint that – as John MacArthur and other dispensationalists have asserted – "There can be no modern apostles." To the contrary, the New Testament speaks of the vital necessity of apostolic anointing, leadership, and direction for the church in all ages. Referring to the Holy Spirit's continual action in raising up apostolic leadership, Greenslade adds: "As Paul makes clear to the Ephesians, it is 'he who ascended far above all the heavens that he might fill all things' who gives 'some to be apostles.' He is building his church still."[52]

It turns out that apostles are the missing link of modern church structure. An analysis of the three main types of structure and government in the modern church – Episcopalianism (hierarchical), Presbyterianism (federal), and Congregationalism (democratic) – reveals that, until quite recently, the apostolic ministry has been almost completely ignored. There a few reasons for this, beginning with the fact that the installment of the bishopric in the second century church meant the end not only of the eldership but the apostleship. Historians Michael Collins and Matthew Price explain the mystery behind the disappearance of the modern apostolate in terms of the so-called "apostolic succession": "The term refers to

---

[50] Peterson, p. 82.

[51] Cited in C. P. Wagner, p. 47.

[52] Greenslade, pp. 139-140.

the fact that the first bishops had been appointed by the apostles and had in their turn appointed successors, who were thus seen as the rightful heirs of the apostles as the senior leaders of the Christian community."[53] Once the bishop was established as the only "apostolic" presence in the church, rejecting the true apostolic function became a simple matter of tradition.

Tradition, along with the spiritual inertia and fear of innovation that result from it, will kill the apostolic movement if not confronted head on. The fact is that the apostolic revelation has been sitting in front of us all along. Perhaps, then, the greatest hindrance to our embracing what C. Peter Wagner terms an "apostolic revolution" is mere pride. The need to "save face" rather than "face the facts" of a long-standing and even embarrassing oversight on the part of the church just may be our biggest hurdle:

> One suspects that behind many fine words too much is at stake for anyone to admit we might have been wrong. There is an alternative. It is not an innovation. We assert as our starting point what the other viewpoints deny: that the apostolic role is as vital and valid today as ever before.[54]

There are other psychological reasons for denying apostleship. Somehow the term "apostle" has become synonymous with "the twelve," and therefore synonymous with spiritual superstardom. (As if the church really had an aversion to superstars in ministry! The refusal of today's mega-pastors to embrace apostleship on the grounds of not wanting to appear boastful seems to me a case of disobedience posing as humility.) Of course, Paul himself is the most vivid example of the principle of apostleship moving beyond the particular historical criterion of physical proximity to Jesus.

---

[53] Michael Collins and Matthew A. Price, *The Story of Christianity: 2,000 Years of Faith* (New York: DK Publishing, 1999), p. 39.

[54] Greenslade, pp. 142-143.

And Paul had no problems with false modesty: "For I consider that I am not at all inferior to the most eminent apostles" (2 Cor. 11:5).

While thus maintaining his equal status with the twelve as an apostle, he nevertheless has to confess: "Christ Jesus came into the world to save sinners, of whom I am chief" (1 Tim. 1:15). So much for the theory of apostolic spiritual giants, gurus or superstars. Whatever apostles may be, they are still beset by sin just like the rest of us. And they are not always big names or high profile people. Other than New Testament scholars, scarcely anyone has ever heard of, say, Junia and Andronicus (Rom. 16:7). Besides, Paul and the other apostles were distinctively team players, and therefore had no need and no desire to somehow make a name for themselves.

But there is another, more practical explanation for the lack of apostles today. It is arguably much easier to take over leadership of an existing church assembly and simply maintain it, than it is to go out and build the church from nothing but faith. Pioneering a host of new churches in a new region, overseeing entire teams of missionaries, or establishing a new move of God is never easy. In many respects, apostleship is synonymous with hardship (2 Tim. 2:3). In terms of church government, however, the disappearance of the apostolic mantle may be the single greatest void of leadership in the modern church. The history of the Corinthian church, and of a number of modern churches, demonstrates that apart from the influence of the founding apostle, the man who personally sat in as midwife in God's birthing process, congregations led by professional preachers will quickly fall into charismatic confusion and political squabbling.

It is precisely the failure of those with an apostolic calling to rise up and assert themselves that has left us with the modern pastorate. The "pastor" of today therefore performs a curious double duty: In the absence of apostles, he exercises apostolic authority over the church – correcting, rebuking, and setting in order – and at the same time he maintains the tender care and oversight of the shepherd as steward of God's heritage. Certainly this oversight has its limitations. I have heard some excellent sermons over the years addressing the real and universal problem of spiritual "blind spots." This problem applies especially to a pastor leading the church with no help from his brethren. How much can one man see?

VI. Prophets, Evangelists and Teachers

Delight is to him, who gives no quarter in the truth, and kills, burns, and destroys all sin though he pluck it out from under the robes of Senators and Judges.

-- Herman Melville, *Moby Dick*

Preach the word! Be ready in season and out of season. Convince, rebuke, exhort, with all longsuffering and teaching.

-- 2 Timothy 4:2

THERE REMAINS ANOTHER class of leaders whose callings I am lumping together for the sake of brevity: the preachers. At first glance this might seem a false distinction since most of the afore-mentioned leaders are involved in preaching the gospel. Indeed, all Christians are called by Jesus Himself to a ministry of proclamation: "Go into all the world and preach..." (Mark 16:15). But unlike apostles, elders, and other church leaders, prophets, evangelists and teachers are set apart for no other purpose. Their primary function is to declare the Word of God to others. They are designated as specific categories of leadership in the church twice in the New Testament (Eph. 4:11, 12; 1 Cor. 12:28. Paul makes no mention of evangelists to the Corinthians, perhaps because their office is so closely related, in certain respects, to that of the apostles, the "sent ones": "Missionaries are evangelists, as being essentially preachers of the Gospel" – *Vine's Dictionary,* "Evangelist," p. 44).

These three offices have been obscured in recent years by the predominance of the pastor in most church settings. The pastor is considered not only a shepherd, but a prophet (he is free to give words of knowledge and prophecy), an evangelist (he gives the soul-winning altar call at the end of the service) and a teacher (he often gives the Sunday school lesson himself). And as we have seen throughout this study, there is inarguably some biblical justification for functional overlap. Paul instructed Timothy, an apostle, to "do the work of an evangelist" (2 Tim. 4:5). Philip was a deacon as well as an evangelist. And pastors are by all means called to preach.

The problem is that pastors typically take on the entire gamut of leadership functions in the church – which means either that the pastor must be, as Howard Snyder has noted, "a superstar," of the church is not receiving or experiencing what it should through the varied ministries and gifts in the New Testament. Still, pastors decry the phenomenon of "spectator Christianity," failing to notice that by reinforcing a visible minister-laity distinction they are its chief proponents. Snyder insists that the problem has everything to do with structure:

> An emphasis on spiritual gifts means church structure which is dynamic, interactive, and organic. It means a conscious resistance to secular organizational models for the church as community. The structure of the community must be based on biblical models.... In many cases a proper emphasis on spiritual gifts means a fundamental rethinking of structure.[55]

One of these gifts is that of the prophet. Prophets are a rare breed to begin with, but in the modern era they are nearly extinct. I have no doubt that prophets still abound, either in relative ignorance of their own gifting, or willingly suppressing it – keeping their gift in the closet, so to speak – in order to comply with the present church format. (In one former church of mine, men with a prophetic gifting had but one chance to let loose with a word from God: the split second between the final note of the last altar call song and the

---

[55] Howard Snyder, *The Problem of Wineskins: Church Structure in a Technological Age* (Downer's Grove, IL: Intervarsity, 1975), p. 126.

final word by the pastor to the congregation. Even then, the pastor had perfect liberty to cut off the prophecy at any time – which was usually taken to mean that it "really wasn't God." But on the other hand, in most churches there are no prophecies at all.)

Whereas apostles exercise considerable authority, and are ready to apply it, prophets seem almost indifferent to authority – at least in human terms. Because they are specifically called to reveal the timely mysteries of God to people temporarily blinded by ignorance, indifference, deception and discouragement, they are not afraid to confront even the highest-ranking of apostles with the truth. They are oblivious, even scornful, of peer pressure and social standards. John the Baptist lived in near isolation, wore bizarre clothing, had a strange diet, and didn't really care what anyone may have thought about it. By the anointed witness of the Holy Spirit, a prophet warned Paul of severe trials awaiting him in Jerusalem:

> And as we stayed many days, a certain prophet named Agabus came down from Judea. When he had come down to us, he took Paul's belt, bound his own hands and feet, and said, "Thus says the Holy Spirit, 'So shall the Jews at Jerusalem bind the man who owns this belt, and deliver him into the hands of the Gentiles" (Acts 21:10, 11).

This was something Paul obviously did not want to hear. He was determined to preach the gospel in Jerusalem, and perhaps was believing God to spare him the usual ordeal of riots and imprisonment. Unlike almost every other Christian convert in the region, Agabus was not the least bit intimidated by the mighty apostle. Thus, like Jeremiah of old, prophets proclaim the truth – whether uplifting or unsettling, politically correct or in complete violation of church traditions and protocols. Wiersbe contrasts the comfortable, predictable ministry of false prophets with the confrontational, provocative message of those who speak in the name of the Lord:

The false prophet is a peddler of cheap alloy, but the prophet is an assayer who turns on the heat so he can test the metal and take away the dross. He is a physician who exposes the ugly sores before he applies the medicine. He is, in short, a person who creates problems by revealing problems so that he can solve problems.[56]

When entire churches are taken in by the schemes of the devil, it is the prophets alone who are willing to stand completely against the tide of opinion and declare the word of God.

By their very nature, prophets are an odd lot. They live eccentric, often ascetic lives. The few men I've met whom I would consider prophets are, to be frank, pretty strange birds. Many times they are the children of poverty or rejection, like Amos and Jeremiah, who are so accustomed to unpopularity that they simply are no longer afraid of it. In any case, the church needs its share of prophets. Prophets stand not at the top of the heap but outside the circle. Their primary function is to call attention to what no one else has yet noticed. The prophet is the meteorologist of the kingdom, who makes prescient forecasts inspired by divine revelation. Unlike the more pragmatic pastor, the prophet sees the future consequences of present decisions based on eternal principles. Though in the context of discussing instinctual perceptions versus cold "objectivity" in science, Isabelle Stengers' comments on the court jesters of old speak pertinently to the ministry of the church "boat rocker," the prophet:

> Since the jester did not speak on behalf of any respectable body, he was able with impunity to draw attention to abuses which the king should suppress, to raise uncertain matters in an admonishing tone, to be receptive to things which the established authorities were either unwilling or unable to see. The contrast is thus between the perception of the jester and the

---

[56] Wiersbe, p. 67.

knowledge of the authorities... Perceptiveness...deals with problems which as yet have no significance but which acquire significance in the future.[57]

Just as the jester was the only voice which could speak unvarnished truth to the king, so the prophets today are called to challenge false teachers, money-grubbing evangelists, and pampered pastors to see themselves in the mirror of God's Word and repent. Such a task calls for men of integrity with deep-seated convictions of the Word of God, willing to confront the most exalted of potentates in order to heal the nation. Consequently, the true prophet has yet to win a church popularity contest. In fact, the history of prophetic ministry in the Old Testament is largely a clash of truth and authority:

> Addressing the kings of Israel usually meant confronting them, for in the eyes of the prophets, the purposes of the kings and their minions were generally inimical to the integrity of the people and contrary to the will of God. As a result, much of the preexilic prophetic literature is sharply critical, negative, and judgmental.[58]

The same holds true today. Greenslade observes simply that "the prophet will be an uncomfortable man." When eventually all hell literally breaks loose in the appointed time of Tribulation on earth, there will remain but a single pair of prophets who will still have the boldness to declare the message of God to a cynical, unbelieving, violently dehumanized world. These prophets have an unmistakably supernatural anointing: "These have power to shut

---

[57] Isabelle Stengers, "Order Through Chaos," cited in Tom Peters, *Thriving on Chaos* (New York: Alfred A. Knopf, 1988), p. 391.

[58] James M. Ward, *Thus Says the Lord: The Message of the Prophets* (Nashville: Abingdon, 1991), p. 23.

heaven, so that no rain falls in the days of their prophecy; and they have power over waters to turn them to blood, and to strike the earth with plagues, as often as they desire" (Rev. 11:6). Here then is a prophet's reward: the power and presence of God upon his life and ministry.

The evangelist also enjoys a specific ministry from God. Evangelists are men of encouragement, gifting and grace who have a knack for winning others to Jesus. They are preachers of a specific sort of message – the *good news*, the gospel of Christ. This is yet another area of ministry that the pastor would be advised to relinquish, because evangelists, like pastors, have a particular gift. If anyone has the authority to address this subject, it is Billy Graham. He notes in the preface to his autobiography, *Just As I Am*:

> In the Bible, an evangelist is a person sent by God to announce the Gospel, the Good News; he or she has a spiritual gift that has never been withdrawn from the Church. Methods differ, but the central truth remains: an evangelist is a person who has been called and specially equipped by God to declare the Good News to those who have not yet accepted it..... [T]he calling of the evangelist is very specific.[59]

The evangelist is the "positive thinker" of the church, who believes against all odds and appearances that anyone can get saved and that everyone in the church has something vital to contribute. Just when the church is beginning to look something like a correctional facility, the evangelist comes along and literally has something good to say to everyone.

As opposed to the prophet, whose unction derives from his love of raw truth, the evangelist is anointed to "preach the gospel to the poor;" i.e., he loves people even more than proper theology. Evangelists may occasionally preach about sin, death, and judgment, like all good preachers do, but somehow we can sense the

---

[59] Billy Graham, *Just As I Am* (New York: Harper, 1997), p. xvii.

whole time that God still loves us and salvation and healing are still available. They often have a ministry of healing with its roots in a strong compassion for hurting, rejected people. In an age of seemingly incurable cynicism, pessimism and unbelief, the evangelist is a breath of fresh air from the Holy Spirit.

Finally, there are the teachers, who are really underrated because their ministry has become so common. Many if not most believers feel they are capable of a teaching ministry, for no other reason than that they've read the New Testament (or at least most of the "key passages"). But having read the Bible does not qualify a man to teach it. Instructing others to learn the truth of God's Word is a gift requiring much labor, patience, and insight into human nature. Teachers must provide a network of revelation. That is, they must link New Testament with Old, link Scripture with experience, and link past history with present reality – and all the while make it interesting. Practically speaking, it means that teachers invest much effort into what seems a small payoff. No one is going to break out into spontaneous worship because someone identified the woman riding the beast in Revelation 17 or explained the gifts of the Spirit or the various pieces of equipment comprising the armor of faith. But when Christians wield their spiritual armor instinctively in the heat of battle, they should realize that at one time they *learned* that from someone somewhere.

It is one thing to win souls; it is another to bring them to maturity in the truth of God's Word. Therefore, as Greenslade affirms, the ministry of teaching is critical to the long-term strength and stability of the church:

> The teacher's aim is to nourish the life of God implanted in others until it blossoms into confident openness before God and the world, able to bear whatever fruit God intends it to produce. In short it is clear that in the New Testament the specific aim of the ministry of the word is to bring believers to maturity.[60]

---

[60] Greenslade, p. 155.

A church on the cutting edge of evangelism, baptized in the Holy Spirit, zealous for good works, but ignorant of the essential doctrines of the faith will eventually fall into one form of deception or another, "carried about with every wind of doctrine, by the trickery of men, in the cunning craftiness of deceitful plotting" (Eph. 4:14). The ministry of teachers immersed in the truth will go a long way towards preventing the sort of spiritual shipwreck that would inevitably result from a false, unbalanced or distorted gospel. Such ministry involves a commitment to the whole truth and nothing but the truth: "For I have not shunned to declare to you the whole counsel of God," said Paul to the elders of the Ephesian church (Acts 20:27).

It is not immediately clear how all this relates to structure. And again there are no strict guidelines. Most churches have their share of prophets, whether the churches (or the prophets) realize it or not. Their prophetic gift should be encouraged and developed throughout the body of Christ, as well as in the local congregation: "Let two or three prophets speak, and let the others judge" (1 Cor. 14:29). To an extent, teachers are preachers and vice-versa. Some would argue that the "teachers" of Ephesians 4 are actually the pastors, men referred to by Paul in the original language as "pastor-teachers." There is certainly biblical support for this view, as Paul told Timothy of elders who "labor in the word and doctrine" (1 Tim. 5:17).

If indeed there is a distinction between the pastoral and teaching ministries, it seems to rest upon the slight difference between moral exhortations and the doctrines and practical outworkings of the faith. To put it another way: Preachers speak to the conscience, teachers to the intellect. But again we should hesitate to draw any sharp lines:

At this point pastors need to be prophetic and prophets pastoral. Pastors whose sensitivity makes them loath to confront and prone to fudge the issue need the prophetic determination to set truth in people's minds in order to free them. Prophets eager to burst in with a "thou art the man" rebuke will check themselves and seek the tact and discrimination of the Holy Spirit.[61]

While teachers abound, good ones are hard to find. Paul's first instruction to Timothy in Ephesus was not to hold an evangelistic meeting or a healing crusade, but to set in order matters of doctrine: "Remain in Ephesus that you may charge some that they teach no other doctrine" (1 Tim. 1:3). This tactic was necessary because there were too many amateurs running around, "desiring to be teachers of the law, understanding neither what they say nor the things which they affirm" (v. 7).

The modern megachurch movement, with its overwhelming emphasis on materialism and largeness of experience, is one indication of many that the church still has a great need for teachers of truth. Other theological trends in the church that call for correction include humanism, evolutionary naturalism, the spiritual subjectivism and moral relativism of the "emergent church" movement, and of course, various forms of those same old heresies that seem to never go away: legalism and Gnosticism.

Yet again we see that the various leadership gifts distributed to the church never reside in a single individual. The rise of leaders in the early church demonstrates that no one man had a very good handle on the manifold ministries of the church of God:

> If the Apostle's work was primarily that of founding Christian churches, those of the prophet and teacher were the proclamation of the divinely inspired message. The exact shade of difference between prophet and teacher is impossible to discover. All, however, were charismatic men.... The worst of sins was to refuse to hear the Spirit speaking through them.[62]

---

[61] Greenslade, p. 161.

[62] Walker, p. 40.

VII. Between Control and Chaos: Striking a Biblical Balance

I am never quite sure that those who are loudest in their approval of the Declaration of Independence would be among the revolutionists to-day, or that those who talk most insistently about patriotism would have been among those whom they love to call the "patriots of '76." Are we consistent in glorifying revolution in the past and abhorring it in the present...?

-- Charles M. Andrews, *The Colonial Background of the American Revolution*

Stand fast therefore in the liberty by which Christ has made us free, and do not be entangled again with a yoke of bondage.

-- Galatians 5:1

REMARKABLE AS IT MAY seem, the Founding Fathers of our nation actually had a better understanding of human nature than do most pastors and leaders in the church today. The framers of the Constitution realized that even a people thoroughly united in their commitment to freedom would ultimately disintegrate without a form of government to match. It wasn't enough for them that the colonists were, to a man, opposed to the abuses of the monarchy. They had seen enough, experienced enough, and knew enough of British imperial history to know that the problem of oppression could not be reduced to the personality of the king, but to a system of government that permitted royal whims and fancies to become law. Freedom could not be ensured by simply finding the best man for the job, because even the best of men can be corrupted.

Drawing from the lessons of history, a humanistic belief in rationalism, and an unprecedented level of scholarly research, open discussion, and heated editorial debate, the Fathers finally ratified the Constitution of 1787. Exactly why it was written was declared clearly in the Preamble:

> We the People of the United States, in order to form a more perfect Union, establish Justice, insure domestic tranquility, provide for the common defense, promote the general Welfare, and secure the blessings of Liberty to ourselves and our Posterity, do ordain and establish this Constitution for the United States of America.

What distinguished the Constitution of the United States from those of other nations was its unique and careful treatment of the concept of governing authority, specifically the *separation of powers*. Whereas peoples before had declared certain acts of presidents, kings, and other rulers to be illegal, they had never managed to control the power of central government to simply revise or overrule the law by amendment or by royal decree. The framers of the Constitution focused therefore not merely on the justness of laws but on the distribution of authority. Power in the United States is spread evenly throughout the nation – from the President to the people. Even then, the Constitution is stretched to its limits (and occasionally beyond them) by power seekers. One can only imagine, for instance, what kind of havoc would be wreaked upon our nation if Presidents like Richard Nixon or Bill Clinton were not held in check by opposition in the House and Senate.

What does all this have to do with the church? More than one might suspect. Our nation was founded on the heels of revolution. As Donald E. Miller concludes in his study of church structure leading into the new millennium, the church is currently in the throes of a similar revolution, actually an extension of Luther's Reformation:

I believe we are witnessing a second reformation that is trans-
forming the way Christianity will be experienced in the new
millennium.... This reformation, unlike the one led by Martin
Luther, is challenging not doctrine but the medium through
which the message of Christianity is articulated.[63]

Given that reformation (literally *re-formation*) requires a support-
ing structure, it should come as no surprise that – as Charles Ryrie
has stated in reference to hierarchical structures – "this form of
government is not found in the New Testament."[64] God loves his
people too much to give them over to the leadership of a single
man, who may or may not abuse them.[65] Nonetheless, old para-
digms die hard. The old "Super-pastor" paradigm will not go away
quickly or easily due to two realities of life in the church: the pastoral fondness for power and position (and the income associated
with them), and the relative ignorance of the average Christian. Let
it be understood that many shepherds now enjoying a life of auton-
omy and luxury on the backs of their sheep will not give it up
without a fight.

On the other hand, some well-meaning believers seem to think
that because everyone in the church loves God and loves his people, there will be no abuse, division, rebellion or deception within

---

[63] Miller, p. 11.

[64] Ryrie, p. 146.

[65] Moses in the Old Testament is an apparent exception. However, not
only was his leadership reserved for the nation of Israel (and thus not
entirely relevant to a discussion of New Testament church structure),
his was a unique calling and ministry: "But since then there has not
arisen in Israel a prophet like Moses, whom the Lord knew face to
face" (Deut. 34:10). Many pastors nonetheless claim to have an
authority equal to that of Moses, so that anyone who crosses them in
any way is in danger of the hazards experienced by Miriam, Korah,
Dathan, Abiram, etc.

it. But this is wishful thinking. Jesus' commentary on the unjust steward speaks to the wisdom of moral, not merely monetary, accountability: "The sons of this world are more shrewd in their generation than the children of light" (Luke 16:8). There is no point, after all, in having ministry requirements that leaders cannot treat the church with contempt, unless such leaders understand that otherwise they might just lose their place in the church – if not their paycheck.

At the same time pastors and elders must have the liberty to preach the Word of God without fear of retribution by an angry or unspiritual congregation. The key is balancing authority and accountability in love and the fear of God. Pastors ruling over congregations often claim that they are accountable to God alone. As we have seen, this is contrary to both the spirit and the letter of the New Testament. Paul encouraged the entire church to be continually "submitting to one another in the fear of God" (Eph. 5:21). The apostle John drew up a basic litmus test for those who claim to love God: "If someone says, 'I love God,' and hates his brother, he is a liar; for he who does not love his brother whom he has seen, how can he love God, whom he has not seen?" (1 John 4:20). I would ask a similar question of those who consider themselves above human accountability: "He who refuses to submit to his brother, whom he has seen, how can he claim to submit to God, whom he has not seen?"

All this having been said, the larger question remains: Just what is the ideal structure for a New Testament church? My answer is: I'm not certain. (My contention all along has been that no one has all the answers; so I'm hoping no one will object if I don't have them all myself.) Nonetheless, in the next few pages I will propose some recommendations for structure and government based on the various indicators provided in the New Testament.

Closely related to organizational structure, firstly, are issues of physical locale and logistics. The early disciples apparently were quick to wean themselves off the tradition of worship exclusively in the temple and synagogue. Indeed the book of Acts seems to emphasize the rather unstructured, informal nature of their meetings just a short time after the outpouring of the Spirit at Pentecost: "So continuing daily with one accord in the temple, *and breaking bread from house to house*, they ate their food with gladness and simplicity of heart" (Acts 2:46). Following the martyrdom of Stephen in Acts 7 and the spreading persecution at Jerusalem led by Saul in Acts 8, church activity in the temple evidently ceases altogether.

Although Paul, following his own conversion, and the other apostles continued to preach in the synagogues of various cities, the churches are thereafter started typically in houses: the house of Lydia in Philippi (Acts 16:40), the house of Jason in Thessalonica (Acts 17:5), the house of Justus in Corinth (Acts 18:6-8). In his letter to the Romans Paul encourages believers to "greet the church that is in their house," in reference to his old friends Priscilla and Aquila (Rom. 16:5). In Colossians Paul requests that believers greet Nympha at Laodicea, and "the church that meets in her house" (Col. 4:15). And on it goes.[66]

Leadership in these local churches seems to have begun with the appointment, or at minimum the *recognition*, of the elders by the apostles (Acts 14:23; Titus 1:5). We have already seen from Scripture and history that the early church had no single presiding bishop. Some might object to this on the grounds of practicality, tradition, or even common sense. None of these should take precedence over the model of the New Testament. And on this particular aspect of church structure the New Testament is clear.

Shared leadership does not mean that no one among the elders can rise up to take charge, or that no one is allowed to lead in any sense. What it means is that the elders, as a group, are jointly responsible for oversight of the congregation. They are free to work among themselves as they see fit. This is not as crazy as it may sound. For instance, juries often select a foreman to help lead and

---

[66] This chapter's review of the "house to house" pattern that really defines how and where the New Testament church gathered is taken largely from Fenn, *Return of the First Church*, pp. 39-49.

organize their decision-making process. But the foreman is there strictly to make the process more efficient. He cannot manipulate the other jurors, nor does he have more than a single vote in the final decision. He represents the rest of them, just as they represent the people. The Houses of Congress, in similar fashion, vote for their whips, speakers, and majority and minority leaders.

It would be best if these elders were appointed by the apostle, that is, the man responsible for the birth of the church itself. (If that man also happens to be the current pastor, he should appoint elders to lead alongside him, or better yet, to lead in his place while he goes off to pioneer new works elsewhere.) The elders should handle the bulk of the duties of counseling, and organizing church activity. They would also share the pulpit (1 Tim. 5:17), so that the congregation could hear the Word from various perspectives, and so that no single preacher could monopolize the ministry. Elders should also be encouraged to ready themselves for apostolic ministry, i.e., to go out and begin other churches. Their replacements in turn should be appointed from within the congregation, whether from the group of deacons or from among other ministers in the church. Their requirements as elders are listed in 1 Timothy 3:1-7.

Deacons would be selected by the church, most feasibly through a vote, perhaps on a yearly or biannual basis (c.f. Acts 6:2, 3). They would be in charge of ministry to the poorer classes and of handling disputes between brethren. They would be granted a specified allotment of the church budget to give at their discretion to those in need. All available funds would come from the working members of the church itself by the usual method of taking up regular offerings. In matters of conflict involving the elders and members of the church, or irreconcilable difficulties between members of the church, deacons would be called in to mediate. If one or both parties are unsatisfied, the deacons would consult with the elders, who would bring the matter formally to the church body for resolution at a prearranged meeting, with the disputing parties as well as all the deacons and elders present. Deacons would also shoulder the bulk of visitation to the sick, the imprisoned, and the elderly.

Exactly how many elders or deacons to appoint is not specified, but is left to the discretion of the apostles. Let us assume for a moment that the number of disciples – active, involved believers – in the church in Acts 6 was somewhere around 240. (This is double the 120 of Acts 2, given steady but less than explosive growth in the intervening period. Despite great miracles and confessions of faith among the multitudes, few actually "dared join them," Acts 5:13.) If the church was 240 strong when the six deacons were appointed, it would mean that deacons were chosen at about one per forty church members. These sorts of numbers would facilitate relatively close-knit fellowship among the deacons and the disciples they served.

Elders might constitute a slightly smaller number, perhaps one for every fifty members, or five elders in the same assembly of believers described above. (An odd number of elders would help prevent gridlock in cases of divided opinion among themselves.) Another line of reasoning would say that since the apostle to deacon ratio in Acts is 12/6, and since elders are appointed as leaders in the place of apostles, there should also be twice the number of elders to deacons where no apostles are present.

The larger church, as mentioned, would decide three specific issues: the appointment of deacons; the resolution of long standing or unreconciled relational conflicts; and discipline by removal (after repeated warnings by leadership) of those continuing in sexual sin or causing divisions (Acts 6:2; Matt. 18:17; 1 Cor. 5:1-5; Rom. 16:17). In this way the church would have a say in matters vital to her own interests under Christ, while at the same time subject to the authority of the elders and apostles. How this would be done is not specified, but one plausible method would be to call a church-wide meeting (something like a political town hall meeting) to be directed by the elders, in which church members could debate the issues and then bring the matter to a vote. Other ministries in the church would be free to function under the oversight of the elders. Again, in the case that elders prove difficult or unreasonable, deacons would be summoned for resolution.

Apostles would maintain contact with the churches, to appoint elders and ensure its continued growth in knowledge, faith and unity (Acts 15:36). Apostles would also be free to visit the churches at their discretion, and would, as the founders of those churches, be entrusted with authority to advise, correct and chasten them (unless and until their testimony becomes compromised, in which case a fellow apostle, or even a recognized prophet, would be called in to help with resolution). Evangelists would be invited by the elderships of various churches to minister grace and encouragement and help generate conversions. It's not clear just where prophets and teachers would come in, although in many churches they already function in a limited capacity within the local church body. Having the witness and blessing of the apostles, they would be granted occasional, perhaps even regular, times to minister to the church (Eph. 4:11, 12; 1 Cor. 12:28, 29).

Sketchy as it is, the preceding structural scenario is clearly preferable to the traditional hierarchical, federal, and congregational forms of church government. The hierarchical model denies the authority of the eldership and the church; the federal ("Presbyterian") model denies apostolic authority; and the congregational model denies all authority in leadership. These are potentially serious matters. It could be argued that to the extent these forms deny the authority vested in the various elements of the church in the Scripture, they resist the authority of the Word of God. Moreover, few modern churches have seriously attempted to incorporate the gifts of the Spirit into the church while maintaining a commitment to order, structure, unity and properly delegated authority.

One glaring potential weakness of the biblical model is that the church is prone to factionalism. It was a pragmatic concern for unity that prompted the second-century bishop Ignatius to establish the local bishop as the uncontested leader of the local church: "He argued strongly that there should be one 'bishop' in charge of each congregation, in order to prevent splits in the church and to ensure that correct beliefs were preserved"[67] (Notice that he didn't argue

---

[67] Michael Smith, "Ignatius of Antioch," from *Eerdman's*, p. 80.

strongly on the basis of Scripture.) It may seem reasonable to leave all authority in the hands of the local pastor, in order to maintain such "unity."

On this, it should be noted that the apostles did not oppose factions with a unity to be enforced by allegiance to the pastor, but with admonitions to the church as a body. Unity in the Bible is a condition in which believers willingly agree to believe and behave according to certain standards. The Corinthians, for example, were divided over the issue of apostolic leadership, some preferring Paul, other Apollos and Peter. Rather than reveal who was the apostle with the highest authority, or assert his own, Paul reminded them that the leader of the church is Jesus, in whom they all believed: "Was Christ divided? Was Paul crucified for you?" (1 Cor. 1:13).

Ironically, the imposition of pastoral authority upon the church does not ensure unity, but creates two distinct, pronounced factions: (1) the pastor and his cronies; and, (2) everyone else in the church. These simmering factions often produce all-out church splits. While there are many admonitions in Scripture for the church to be united, there are no admonitions to the bishops or elders to make sure that it takes place. In fact, local shepherds and leaders are reminded frequently not to "lord it over" others (Mark 10:42, 43; Luke 22:25, 26; 1 Pet. 5: 1-3). Paul assured the Corinthians that even legitimate apostolic authority had its limitations: "Not that we have dominion over your faith" (2 Cor. 1:24). Unity is the job of the entire church.

I will be the first to admit that much of the preceding flies in the face of tradition, even of sensibility. But then, so does much of the Christian life generally. It is not practical or reasonable to give up addictions, tell the truth when a little white lie would make everything easier, or stop fooling around outside marriage *altogether*. It is not sensible for any of us to commit *unconditionally* to an invisible God for the rest of our lives, if necessary to the point of death. Worldly cynics scoff at the notion of loving one's enemies, much less blessing and praying for them. And there are few economic experts who would advocate giving sacrificially on a tight budget. Jesus was committed to the Father and the Word of God, regardless of traditions. So His indictment of the Pharisees ruling over first century Judaism seems to apply just as well to many of the pastors in charge of twenty-first century Christianity:

"All too well you reject the commandment of God, that you may keep your tradition" (Mark 7:9).

Appendix: Meeting House to House

AS MENTIONED IN THE LAST chapter, the early church at some point after Pentecost broke from the tradition of worship in the temple and began meeting in homes. We have seen that leaders of the first congregations, in cities like Corinth and Thessalonica, were appointed by the apostles and shared their duties alongside others. We have also seen that believers in the early church meetings exercised a wide diversity of gifts of the Spirit in order to edify the church as a whole. But admittedly very little has been said of what these meeting may have looked like – or what they should look like today.

For those interested in doing house church a host of questions present themselves, having to do with leadership, logistics, organization, doctrine, giving and finances, interaction with other churches, outreach and evangelism, and doubtless many others. What I intend to focus on here, however, are the principles operating behind the house church meeting itself, patterned after the New Testament.

Probably the most useful New Testament book for getting a handle on practical church dynamics is 1 Corinthians. Having established a sort of "division of labor" in the church in Chapter Twelve ("many parts, one body"), and the spiritual preeminence of love in Chapter Thirteen, Paul begins to break down some practical issues of holding a church meeting in Chapter Fourteen:

[26] "How is it then, brethren? Whenever you come together, each of you has a psalm, has a teaching, has a tongue, has a revelation, has an interpretation. Let all things be done for edification. [27] If anyone speaks in a tongue, let there be two or at the most three, each in turn, and let one interpret. [28] But if there is no interpreter, let him keep silent in church, and let him speak to himself and to God. [29] Let two or three prophets

speak, and let the others judge. [30] But if anything is revealed to another who sits by, let the first keep silent. [31] For you can all prophesy one by one, that all may learn and all may be encouraged. [32] And the spirits of the prophets are subject to the prophets. [33] For God is not the author of confusion but of peace, as in all the churches of the saints.

[34] Let your women keep silent in the churches, for they are not permitted to speak; but they are to be submissive, as the law also says. [35] And if they want to learn something, let them ask their own husbands at home; for it is shameful for women to speak in church.

[36] Or did the word of God come originally from you? Or was it you only that it reached? [37] If anyone thinks himself to be a prophet or spiritual, let him acknowledge that the things which I write to you are the commandments of the Lord. [38] But if anyone is ignorant, let him be ignorant.

[39] Therefore, brethren, desire earnestly to prophesy, and do not forbid to speak with tongues. [40] Let all things be done decently and in order" (1 Cor. 14:26-40).

Though there are, again, numerous issues to address concerning house church, I believe three important matters in this text call for special attention. First, there is *the need for all to participate*. When Paul says that each part of the body is "necessary" (1 Cor. 12) and each part "does its share" (Eph. 4), he speaks the language of participation. This needs to be mentioned because many of us have come from comparatively stifling church backgrounds in which one man does all the talking. (Indeed, the argument could be made that 1 Cor. 14 simply has no application in most traditional church settings.) In a healthy house church environment, each member has something to contribute; and just as all the parts of the body are essential, so all the gifts of the Spirit are essential. In the text above some teach, some sing, prophesy, interpret, etc., each and all for edification of the body.

Secondly, all things *must be done in order*. Now for years when I read "in order," I thought this meant that things must be *organized and controlled* – that the church service began at a regular time, that there was a predictable order of worship,[68] that the ushers were at the door to greet those entering the building, that the chairs were arranged in the correct pattern, and so on. However, the emphasis here seems to be on mutual respect and courtesy rather than mechanical compliance to a set routine. Paul thus instructs that speaking in tongues be done "each in turn." Similarly, those with a prophetic word are to prophesy "one by one." Each member, then, has to be polite and wait for (better still, *listen to*) the one speaking, and allow him to finish. The Corinthians were apparently an impatient lot, because not only did they have a habit of interrupting one another, but they even cut in line at the Lord's Supper: "For in eating, each one takes his own supper ahead of the others…" (1 Cor. 11:21).

Finally, there must be *mutual respect*. One of the more divisive issues increasingly confronting the church is the role(s) of women in ministry, particularly in leadership. Paul in this text says "Let your women keep silent in the churches." To a modern mind unfamiliar with first century culture that sounds right away like simple gender discrimination. For that reason this is a sore subject for many, women and men alike. Among those most disaffected by the old pastor-as-monarch paradigm, after all, are women with a sincere but suppressed desire to function effectively in the body of Christ. Many observers would agree that the evangelical church, while implicitly encouraging men to "rise up" and pursue leadership, typically restricts women's ministry to secondary roles – in Sunday Schools, nurseries, children's churches, and administrative tasks.

Now I am aware that scholars have interpreted this passage to mean everything from "Women need to shut up in church just like Paul says," to "This is a purely cultural matter restricted to the

---

[68] In most of the churches I ever attended the order of worship ran like clockwork: first, a handful of preselected songs led by a worship team; then announcements; then opening prayer; then a sermon by the pastor; then an altar call; then a closing song; then a closing prayer.

early church in Corinth." And in the interest of disclosure let me say that I am not a professional scholar myself. Nonetheless, a straightforward reading of v. 34-35 in the context of 1 Cor. 14:26-40 suggests to me *initially*, at least, that Paul has the proper recognition of authority in mind, as a means to help maintain proper order in the church. It may be that some of the women were hijacking the meetings by speaking out of turn, interrupting even their own husbands. This is bound to happen from time to time, of course, as words spoken and ensuing discussion sometimes becomes emotionally engaging. But when the meeting becomes disorderly as a result there is confusion (v. 33).

Note that while Paul says "Let your women keep silent in the churches," in the same breath he adds, "they are to be submissive, as the law says." Paul evidently wasn't referring so much to all the women, but the wives, for he adds that they should "ask their husbands at home" when they have questions (presumably questions that might veer the meeting off course and onto "bunny trails," as we like to say in our own house church group). Nor was he saying that the women (married or not) should be *completely silent*, because earlier in the same chapter he expresses his wish that "all prophesy" and that "each of you has a psalm, has a teaching, has a tongue, has a revelation, has an interpretation." Additionally Paul has already mentioned women in the church who do prophesy, in a similar context of doing so while honoring the authority of their husbands (1 Cor. 11:3-5).

However, reputable scholars like Walter Kaiser have suggested an alternative interpretation, that when Paul mentions "the law" in v. 34, seemingly for the purpose of keeping women silent, he actually refers to the Talmud (the "oral law") rather than the Old Testament:

The problem simply put is this: nowhere in the whole Old Testament does it teach or even imply what is claimed here! No law in the entire Old Testament, much less the Torah, can be cited to teach that woman "must be in submission" and "remain silent" and, if she wants to know or ask about anything,

86

she "should ask [her own] husband at home." Women spoke freely in public in both testaments.[69]

With that observation in mind Grenz and Kjesbo add:

Another possibility is that the statements directing women to keep silent represent the teachings of Paul's opponents, which he quotes from the Corinthian correspondence to him. The rhetorical questions (v. 36) introduced by the exclamation "What!" form Paul's refutation of the ban on women's vocal participation in worship.[70]

In other words, some of the Corinthian men were actually citing bits from the Talmud in vv. 34-35 to keep the women "in their place," and Paul chose at this point in the letter (vv. 36-37) to rebut their claim by pointing out that access to the truth of God's word was not limited to a handful of rabbis presuming themselves to be the proper custodians of divine revelation. I lean toward this latter interpretation, not only because nowhere does the Old Testament explicitly command the silence of women, but because it makes better sense of the passage as a whole, with the emphasis on both participation and order.

Of course much has been said on this subject and readers are encouraged to study further.[71] My take on the whole passage is basically this: Each of us should have something to share – women

---

[69] Walter C. Kaiser, Jr., "Correcting Caricatures: The Biblical Teaching on Women,"
http://www.walterckaiserjr.com/womenpage4.html.

[70] Stanley J. Grenz & Denise Kjesbo, *Women in the Church: A Biblical Theology of Women in Ministry* (Downer's Grove, Ill: Intervarsity, 1995), p. 119.

[71] For a more thorough examination of this topic from a house church perspective see Fenn, pp. 166-174.

by all means included – but for that to happen each has to also limit how much they share at any one time. In short, ministry in the New Testament church is marked by both liberty and love. Liberty in the Holy Spirit allows all the members of the body to express the gifts God has given them, and the love of Christ demands that they do so only with due respect for others and reverence for the Lord himself: "submitting to one another in the fear of God" (Eph. 5:21).

Index

Constitution (of the United States), 73-74
counsel, counseling, 18, 46, 70, 78
Davids, Peter H., 20
deacon, 13, 19, 33, 42-44, 46-47, 51-54, 64, 78-79
Declaration of Independence, 24
Dining with the Devil (Guinness), 18, 25
disciple, discipleship, 10, 19, 24, 26-27, 32, 51-52, 76, 79
doctrine, 12, 15, 17-18, 42, 48, 70-71, 75, 83
Douglas, J. D., 54
Dowley, Tim, 45
Drake, Herb, 12
ecclesiastical, ecclesiology, 10, 17-18, 23, 35
Eckhardt, John, 56, 59
Eerdman's Handbook to the History of Christianity (Dowley,
    ed.), 45, 80
elders, eldership, 13, 20, 26, 42-48, 52, 54, 56, 58-59, 63, 70, 76-81
Enroth, Ronald, 41-42
episcopal, Episcopalian, 20, 32, 59
Escape from Church, Inc. (G. Wagner), 31
evangelism, evangelist, 10, 13, 19, 24, 54, 58, 63-64, 67-71, 80, 83
false teacher/prophet, false teaching, 30, 57-58, 65-67
fellowship, 10, 12, 16, 26, 32, 48, 79
Fenn, John, 11, 77, 87
fivefold ministry, 13, 58
gifts of the Spirit, 11-12, 44, 53, 59, 68-71, 80, 84, 88
gospel, 15-16, 36, 56, 58, 63, 65, 68, 70
Gospel (of Matt, Mark, etc.), 18, 34, 53
govern, government, 21-24, 30, 36, 42, 46, 48, 52, 59, 61, 73-76
Graham, Billy, 68
Green, Vivian, 17
Greenslade, Philip, 43, 59-60, 69, 71
Grenz, Stanley J., 87
Guinness, Os, 18, 25-26
Hard Sayings of the Bible (Kaiser, et al), 20
hierarchy, hierarchical, 10, 13, 17, 20, 26-27, 42, 47-48, 59, 75, 80
Hodges, Melvin, 35-36

Moody Monthly, 49

New Testament, 10-11, 13, 18, 20, 21-23, 32-33, 36-37, 42-44, 46-48, 52-53, 56-57, 59, 61, 63-64, 69, 75-77, 83, 88

Old Testament, 21-22, 67, 86-87

organization, organizational, 10-11, 16, 19, 21, 24, 27, 32, 36, 64, 76, 87

Pagan Christianity? (Viola & Barna), 11, 18

pastor, pastoral, 10, 11, 13, 16, 18-23, 25-27, 29-37, 40-48, 52, 56, 60, 61-62, 63-68, 70, 73, 75-76, 78, 81-82, 85

Paul the Apostle: The Triumph of God in Life and Thought (Beker), 58

"Pearlygate," 39

Pentecost, 11, 77, 83

Peters, Tom, 67

Peterson, Jim, 26, 58-59

Pfeiffer, Charles F., 47

Philip, Johnson C., 12

presbyter, Presbyterian, 45, 53, 59, 80

priest, priesthood, 16-18, 22-23, 25, 29

prophecy, prophesy, 18, 63, 65, 67, 84-86

prophet, prophetic, 13, 19, 21-22, 30, 58, 63-68, 70-71, 80, 83-85

reform, (Protestant) Reformation, Reformers, 9, 16-18, 26, 77-75

Reforming the Church Today (Küng), 31

Reinventing American Protestantism: Christianity in the New Millennium (Miller), 27

Return of the First Church (Fenn), 11, 77

revolution, (American) Revolution, 9, 16, 27, 60, 74

Roberts, Oral, 39

Rutz, James, 17, 25

Ryrie, Charles C., 44, 75

salvation, saved, 15-16, 18, 33, 35, 51, 68

Sanders, J. Oswald, 23

servant, servanthood, 19, 22-23, 26-27, 40, 42, 46, 52-54, 79

sheep (as metaphor), 29-32, 43, 75

shepherd, shepherding, 29-31, 36, 42-45, 47-48, 61, 63, 75, 81

Short, Larry, 36

Vine, W.E., 42, 44-45, 63
Vine's Expository Dictionary of New Testament Words, 42, 63
Vineyard Association of Churches, 27, 32
Viola, Frank, 11, 18, 37, 47
Vital Church Issues: Examining Principles and Practices in
	Church Leadership (Zuck), 22
Wagner, C. Peter, 46, 56, 59-60
Wagner, Glenn, 31
Walker, Williston, 21, 71
Ward, James M., 67
Wiersbe, Warren, 39, 66
Wimber, John, 32
women (in ministry), 53, 84-87
Women in the Church: A Biblical Theology of Women in
	Ministry (Grenz & Kjesbo), 87
Wright, David F., 45
Zuck, Roy B., 22, 45

Notes

Notes

Notes

Notes

Notes

Notes